D0209085

DEATH-DEFYING FAITH

The Extraordinary Life of "Miracle Man"
PETER PRETORIUS

by PETER AND ANN PRETORIUS

"When a man dies, a library burns down."

—AFRICAN PROVERB

May this book serve as a library of the amazing,
real-life experiences God has brought
into our lives over the years.

I dedicate this book to my dear Dad, Isak, who shared all my dreams and was the first one to stay over in Mozambique, faithfully labouring on the building of the roadway to what became our Pambara Life Centre, home to many orphans.

To our daughter, Jackie, who excitedly transcribed the original audio into text files.

To our amazing six children, their precious spouses and to our many wonderful grandchildren who are the next generation who can love and carry the vision and mission of this work in their hearts.

CONTENTS

PART I

GOD CALLS AN ADRENALINE JUNKIE

Therefore, if anyone is in Christ, he is a new creation; old things have passed away; behold, all things have become new.

2 CORINTHIANS 5:17

"JESUS CHRIST! I'M GOING TO DIE!"

KYALAMI RACE TRACK, JOHANNESBURG, SOUTH AFRICA, 1970

The hum of the engine. The rumble of the road. The smells of petrol and rubber heating on the pavement. This was the thrill of the race.

And I *loved* it.

Everything was perfect as I turned my Cooper Climax racing car onto the straight. As the adrenaline surged through me, I pushed the pedal to the floor. At 150 miles an hour, the edge of the track flashed by in a blur. That was how I wanted it. I'd never felt so . . . *alive*.

The car had experienced problems ever since I blew an engine during a race in Zimbabwe. But now, with a new engine, she roared like a lion. I had a dream of being a Formula One world champion, and nothing would stop me.

I flew out of the Crowthorne corner and headed into the Jukskei sweep, coming up fast behind a Lotus Super 7. As I came down the hill, the driver indicated that I should pass him on the left, my racing lane.

I steered left and accelerated. "Wait a minute! What is he doing?"

Just as I made my move, he lost control. Smoke billowed from his screeching tyres as he spun crazily, directly in front of me. There was no time to react. No way to miss him. "Jesus Christ!" I yelled. "I'm going to die!" It wasn't a prayer. The name of Jesus was nothing more than a swear word to me. I tensed and prepared myself for the shock of a devastating collision.

Then . . . *nothing*. The next thing I knew, I was in the clear. I don't know how I missed him. Somehow, I had found a gap and narrowly avoided a collision that would likely have killed us both.

Regaining control as I ascended the hill, I turned and pulled into the pit area, too shaken to continue. "Jesus!" I climbed out of my car. "That was scary!" A grin spread across my face. "*And* fun."

That wasn't the first time my thirst for adventure had almost cost me my life. At the age of 24, I searched constantly for the next thrill. By flirting with death, I hoped to find something that would give my life meaning.

Anyone observing from the outside would have thought I had it all, and I suppose I did. But it wasn't enough. Something was missing, and I desperately wanted to find it.

Although I had not yet reached my mid-twenties, I already managed our family's building construction company in Johannesburg, South Africa. I made enough money to do just about anything I wanted to do, including operating my own racecar team.

The thrill of racing that seemed so vibrant in the moment, faded over time. And when that didn't bring me the peace of mind I sought, I tried to find fulfillment by learning how to fly. I took lessons, got my pilot's license, and flew to all my out-of-town meetings. But, as with everything else, the thrill faded.

I threw myself into gambling. For a while, it was exciting to know that hundreds of thousands of dollars could be won or lost on the turn of a card. But the fun and the satisfaction didn't last. Soon, gambling lost its lure, too.

Nothing money could buy filled the empty, uneasy feeling that gnawed at my insides. I was bored, even as I roared down the racetrack at 150 miles an hour. My life was a succession of thrills that lasted for a minute or two, but it seemed to me that in the long run, life had no meaning.

Little did I know defying death would become a staple of my life for years to come . . . a distinct facet of the faith I was yet to discover, and the calling God had in store for my life. But first my life had to be brought to a screeching halt—through a divine event that would change the course of my life forever.

CHAPTER 1

NOTHING SHORT OF A MIRACLE

THE FAMILY FARM, EASTERN LOWVELD, SOUTH AFRICA, 1979

My entire life I'd spun my wheels, taken lap after lap in the same direction, hoped for something different. But one November evening, everything came to a screeching halt the way many life-changing experiences do: with the ringing of a phone.

We were just getting ready for dinner.

"Hello?"

"Peter. It's Mom." Her voice trembled.

"Is everything okay?"

"No."

I braced myself for the worst.

"It's your dad." Her voice broke. "He's had two heart attacks. One here at home, and another in the ambulance on the way to the hospital."

"Is he going to be all right?" *Stupid question.*

Mom took a deep breath. "The doctor doesn't think he'll make it through the next 24 hours. You'd better come quickly if you want to see him alive."

Within a couple of hours, I sat stunned on a flight bound

for Johannesburg. It was the longest one-hour flight I had ever experienced. My heart sat in my throat, and every minute felt like an eternity. Would we ever get there?

As soon as we landed, I rented a car and drove like the race-car driver I'd once been, all the way to the hospital.

I needn't have bothered. Dad was unconscious and on life-support. An oxygen mask covered his pale face. Medication and fluids dripped into his veins. Monitors and gauges beeped and whirred as the nurses and doctors monitored him closely.

My mother sat beside him, her forehead wrinkled in fear, staring at nothing in particular. What would she do without him? What would any of us do without him? He had always been our source of strength.

My healthy, rugged father had travelled up to Johannesburg, some 350km (220 miles) away, to help my brother who also worked in construction. Now my father looked like he was already dead. It took everything within me not to fall to my knees and beg him not to leave.

I found his doctor and asked if there was any hope. I desperately wanted him to say, "He'll be up and around in no time."

He didn't.

"We're doing all we can, but it's unlikely he'll make it through the next several hours," the doctor said. "And if he does survive, his heart has been severely damaged."

He would never lead a normal life again. I believed my strong, hard-working father would rather die than spend his life as an invalid.

My heartache and anxiety was unbearable. What about my

children? How would they cope with the pain of losing their beloved Oupa who always had time for a joke and a story?

I thanked the doctor for his honesty, returned to my rental car and wept like a baby.

SEEDS OF CHRISTIANITY

Until that moment in my car, I didn't think much about God— and I certainly didn't have much good to say about Christians. I thought they were wimps, people who couldn't get their own lives together, so they turned to God for comfort. I had no use for a "pie in the sky" approach to living. Life was to be experienced in the here and now. With a restless spirit and a thrill for adventure, I always tested the limits, ready and willing to experience everything life offered. Besides, I didn't come from a religious family. We weren't anti-religion; we just simply didn't think about God.

The only memorable run-in I'd had with a Christian man was as a nine-year-old boy. I was already a cigarette smoker and proud of it. That's why I was happy to share my expertise with a friend . . . a pastor's son.

My friend went home reeking of tobacco, so it was no surprise that his father quickly caught on to what we were up to. The man marched over to our house and banged on the front door.

My mother ran to see who it was. "I'm coming! I'm coming!" I was right behind her expecting to discover news of some terrible emergency.

When Mom opened the door, there stood the pastor, his

face red and twisted with anger. He glared and pointed at me. "Is this your son?"

"That's right."

"I want you to know right now that this boy will *never* amount to *anything*. He's been *cursed* from the day he was born!"

He didn't stop, and my gentle mother stood there and took the abuse, hatred and condemnation the man poured on us. I knew that what I'd done was wrong, but I didn't deserve to be treated like this, and neither did my wonderful mother. I decided on that day that if this man were a typical Christian, I would have nothing to do with church. And for the next 25 years, I didn't.

But as I sat in the hospital parking lot, weeping bitter tears for my dying father, another distant memory flashed into my mind. I remembered back to when, a few years after that run-in with the pastor, my aunt took my mother and me to an Oral Roberts crusade.

At that crusade, I spent most of the time fascinated not by the Christian man at the podium, but by a man in a wheelchair. His legs were so thin they looked like sticks. They obviously could not support his body.

This man captured my attention because he kept bending his legs, shoving them underneath the cushions on his wheelchair, and doing all sorts of things "normal" people couldn't do. I didn't mean to stare, but it amazed me to see the way he flopped those legs around as if they had no bones in them.

Then, as Oral Roberts prayed for the sick, two fellows pushed this crippled man to the edge of the platform. I remember thinking that the poor fellow was going to go home terribly disappointed. But as soon as the famous evangelist prayed for him, the man jumped out of his wheelchair and ran around in front of the platform. Those rag-doll limbs were suddenly strong, sturdy and normal! I stood there gaping, amazed by what I saw.

That experience resonated with me for weeks, but eventually my mind wandered back to normal preteen concerns like girls, sports and school. I forgot all about it. Forgot about it until years later as I sat in that hospital parking lot. Suddenly, hope surged through me. If God could cause a cripple to jump out of his wheelchair and—not walk, but—*run*, then He could heal my dad's heart.

"WE'VE GOT TO FIND SOME-
ONE TO PRAY FOR DAD."

I dried my eyes, sucked up my resolve and returned to my mother. "We've got to find someone to pray for Dad."

"But who?" We had never even been to church and didn't have a clue who to turn to. Like us, none of the people in our social circle attended church.

Then a thought occurred to me. My aunt who had dragged me to that Oral Roberts crusade . . . she had a son.

"What about Jannie?"

"Your cousin?"

"He always wanted to be a preacher, didn't he?"

My mother looked doubtful. "But do you know how long

it's been since?"

"Fifteen years?"

"More like twenty." She considered the thought. "I'm not sure I have any contact numbers for him."

"We've got to try. Maybe he's still in Pretoria."

We spent the next four hours calling everybody imaginable—anyone who might know where cousin Jannie was. What a relief when we finally heard his voice on the phone. As it turned out, he had completed his theological training in America and returned to pastor a church in Pretoria. He said he would be happy to pray for Dad.

"In fact," he suggested, "why don't we pray right now on the phone?"

Mom and I listened while he calmly and simply asked God to heal my father. After I hung up, I looked at Mom and she looked at me. I don't know what I expected to happen; sparks flying out of the telephone or the arrival of a mighty angel would have been nice. Nothing of the sort took place.

What I didn't know was that as soon as my cousin hung up the telephone, he called the elders of his church and asked them to travel with him to the hospital. As I tossed and turned through a long, sleepless night, those men of faith stood beside my dad's bed, anointed him with oil and asked God to heal him.

MIRACLE MAN

Early the next morning, I drove to the hospital, prepared for the worst. Dread and fear had almost overcome me as I waited for the nurse to let me into the intensive care unit. I half expected her to tell me that my father had died during the night.

Instead, when she opened the door, a smile lit up her face. "Come quickly," she said. "Your father is so much better!"

My heart pounded as I followed her down the corridor to my father's room. He was not only better, he looked completely well. The deathly pallor of the night before had been replaced by a healthy glow on his cheeks. He sat up in bed, breathing easily without an oxygen mask. The drips and lines that had administered fluids and medicine mere hours before were gone. He was hungry—*hungry!*—and waiting for breakfast to arrive.

"Peter, I'm so glad you've come."

Tears welled up in my eyes as my words caught in my throat. "Dad, you look terrific!"

God had responded to our prayers.

That afternoon, the staff moved Dad out of the intensive care unit and into a private ward. A few days later, he walked out of the hospital and returned home. His strength had returned and he was eager to return to work. Anyone who didn't know better would have thought the man had never been ill.

Shortly before his discharge, a professor visited Dad with a group of medical students from the local university. The professor showed his students the medical reports recorded on the day of my dad's heart attacks. Then he showed them the corresponding reports taken after his healing.

Shaking his head in amazement, the professor said, "Three times in my career I have come across things that are totally inexplicable. All I can say is that they are miracles." My father, the Miracle Man.

That was the first time my wife, Ann, and I had ever experienced the supernatural power of God. Little did we know, it was only the beginning.

"HOW COULD THIS HAPPEN?"

Naturally, I wanted to spend as much time with my father as I could, but I owned a tobacco farm, and it was the middle of our tobacco season. We had gathered our first crop and begun the drying process in the barns. Tobacco requires constant attention at that stage.

On the day I knew I had to leave to return home, I struggled to find the words to tell my cousin Jannie how much I appreciated everything that he, and God, had done for my father.

"Jan," I said, "I don't understand why God did this. My dad and I have never done anything for God, and yet He did this wonderful thing for us."

Jannie simply smiled.

Before he left, I said, "If you're ever in our area, and you have some time, please come and visit. I'd like to find out more about why and how God could do such a thing."

Jannie said he would take me up on my invitation, but I didn't think it would ever happen.

I was wrong.

Several weeks later, out of the blue, Jannie arrived on the farm. At that time of year, 18-hour workdays were not uncommon for tobacco farmers. It was close to 11 p.m. when I finally made my way back to the house. Jannie was there waiting with Ann, my wife of only three years, and he wasted no time. He explained that God had given us the most precious gift He could ever give—Jesus. God waited for us to respond by receiving His Son.

It seemed so simple, and yet I had so many questions. How could this be true?

THROUGH ANN'S EYES

Jannie had Peter and I captivated. He told us about the incredible gift of Jesus that God had for us. He asked, "How would you feel if you turned that gift down?"

At once, memories of my grandmother—a role model whom I was named after—flooded my mind. She once said to me, "When are you going to learn how to receive?"

I knew in my heart that this was the answer Peter and I had been searching for all our lives. The discussion continued until Jannie leaned in and asked, "Are you ready to accept this wonderful gift?"

I couldn't stop tears of joy from flowing as God's extravagant love and grace became real to me for the first time. I enthusiastically responded, "Yes!" I was ready, without hesitation.

"And you, Peter?"

But Peter was more methodical. He knew this was such a big decision, and he would not make it lightly. He simply stated, "I need some time to think about it." He told me later that he knew he needed to give himself to God completely, or not at all.

Jannie gently responded, "Please don't put it off. It's so important."

Then Peter excused himself.

I understood his indecision, but I didn't want to wait. Life was tough, and I needed *help!* So when Jannie offered to lead me in a prayer, I wholeheartedly agreed. But there was one problem. "I don't know how to pray," I said. "And besides, I don't have a prayer book."

Jannie smiled. "You don't need a prayer book. You can ask God for anything at any time. He even knows what you are thinking."

That was it. I closed my eyes and prayed awkwardly, asking Jesus to become the Lord of my life. Then I asked God for two things. "Jesus, please help us so that our children don't wait as long as I did to accept You. And don't let my husband sleep until he also makes this decision."

RESTLESS NIGHT

No matter how hard I tried, I couldn't get comfortable in my bed. Although I was exhausted, I tossed and turned. I pondered what Jannie had told us, and I knew he was telling the truth. I had seen the power of Jesus heal a crippled man. I had seen Him bring my father back from the edge of death. And for the first time I saw how everything that had happened in my life had led me to that very moment . . .

CHAPTER 2

HOW MY WORLD FELL APART

JOHANESSBURG, SOUTH AFRICA, 1960–1963

Having migrated from Holland in the mid 1700s, my family was firmly entrenched in South Africa by the time I was born in Johannesburg in 1945.

My father, Isak, was a wonderful man, and I loved him dearly. He was a rugged, tough fellow, about six feet tall, with long, curly hair and a constant bronze tan from working outdoors. I had the type of relationship with my dad that every son would want. We did most things together, including the fun of following sports events like rugby. And as I grew and participated in sports myself, he never missed a single game.

My mother, Jean, was my dad's opposite. There was nothing at all "rugged" about her. She was a refined, petite woman with a lovely smile and a friendly nature. A gentle, nurturing woman, she seldom met anyone she didn't like. If she did, she never let it be known. She was the most positive individual I have ever known.

At first, my early years were idyllic. I had a mom and dad who believed in me, even at times when I didn't deserve to be believed in. My brother, Thys, six years my junior, looked up to me as most younger siblings tend to do. My older sister, Dawn, and I always enjoyed a great relationship. Directly after school, she relocated to Cape Town to attend Helderberg College. To this day, I don't recall ever having an argument with her.

When I was 13 years old, the world around me suddenly changed.

THE SHARPEVILLE MASSACRE

The catalyst for our family's economic downfall was the Sharpeville Riots, otherwise known as the Sharpeville Massacre of 1960. A large group of black youth, protesting the racist government policy regarding identity pass laws, converged on the police station in the town of Sharpeville. There was no evidence that any of the protesters had weapons, but the police opened fire anyway. When the shooting stopped, 69 people had been killed, many of them women and children. One hundred and eighty more were wounded. This was the start of armed resistance in South Africa.

The tragedy started weeks of protests throughout our country. South Africa teetered on the brink of revolution. The economy collapsed. The building trade crashed. My dad was a hard worker who ran his own construction firm. He had done well, but suddenly, it seemed that every building construction project in South Africa ground to a halt. My father quickly found himself in deep financial trouble.

Dad searched for another job, but despite his years of experience and his obvious skills, no one was hiring. Within the space of six months, we lost everything, including our home in one of Johannesburg's most prominent neighbourhoods. For three years, we were so poor we didn't know where our next meal was coming from. I can remember going weeks without a decent meal. At times, we didn't have a single crumb of food in the house.

Ours was the opposite of a "rags-to-riches" story. We went from riches to rags. My family's fall into poverty was swift and steep. Our survival depended on innovation and ingenuity.

Once on the way home from school, I saw a chicken strutting across the road. I still don't know where it had come from, because we lived in a residential neighbourhood in the middle of the city. Nevertheless, there it was, looking plump and delicious. It never occurred to me that the animal might belong to someone. All I knew was that I was hungry, and it had been a long, long time since we'd had anything as tasty as fried chicken.

That poor creature never had a chance. I caught it, rang its neck on the spot, stuck it under my school blazer and carried it home. We had chicken for dinner that night.

During those lean days, I learned that when people are desperate, they'll do just about anything to survive. My mother had taught us good moral values and expected us to live by them. She raised us not to steal, lie or disrespect other people's property. Yet I soon ventured out during the middle of the night to steal dairy products from people's porches after the local milk truck had made its deliveries. Mom must have known I was stealing the milk we had for breakfast every morning, but she never asked where it came from.

When the electricity supplier turned off our lights, my dad rigged a temporary power supply to our home. I don't know how he got away with it, but somehow he did.

He wasn't so lucky with the water company though. When he tried to bypass their system, they caught on and removed a section of pipe to stop the flow of water into our house. For two years, we had no running water.

Every night after our neighbour turned off his lights, I climbed the fence, attached a garden hose to his outside water tap and filled every pot, basin and tub that we had with water. The only difference between us and millions of other poor African families, was that we didn't need to walk four or five miles every day to get water. All we had to do was go next door and hope that no one came running out with a shotgun. Another difference was that the water we got from our neighbour was not filled with deadly bacteria, as is the case for many in Africa. They walk for hours, only to bring home water jars full of disease and death.

Sadly, although things were bad for the Pretorius family, they were about to get worse.

Shortly after my dad's business collapsed, my mom was diagnosed with lupus, a painful and debilitating disease. She spent several weeks in the hospital, some of the time in a coma. I was terribly frightened that we might lose her. My mother was the one person in the world who could never find fault in me. While trying my hand at doing laundry and ironing shirts, I came to appreciate all she did for us each day.

Every morning, I'd walk an hour and 45 minutes to school because I didn't have money for the bus. After school, I'd walk to the hospital to see my mom, and then I'd walk home, a total distance of 17 miles.

This is another way in which I gained an understanding of what life is like for millions of African people. Sometimes visitors will ask me why Africans walk so much. My answer is, "What else can they do?" If it takes every cent you have to put food on the table, then how do you pay for transport? People in Africa do what they need to do to get by. For many of them that includes walking 15 or 20 miles every day.

I felt the weight of responsibility settle on my shoulders. With my dad struggling to find work, Thys still a young boy and Dawn at college, I tried to fill the gaps. Thankfully, my mother regained enough of her strength to return home, although she was never completely well after that. She brought with her a large supply of appetite suppressant tablets that her doctor had given her to counter the effects of the cortisone treatment that caused her to retain fluids and gain weight. On more than one occasion, she shared her medicine with the rest of us so we wouldn't be so hungry. That's how poor we were.

Then, we received news that all our possessions were going to be reclaimed in order to settle our debts. Creditors planned to take our car, our furniture and anything else that could be sold. To prepare for this, I had some fun. Thys and I spent several hours doing things our parents had never allowed us to do. We jumped on the beds as if they were trampolines, and leaped from the bedroom wardrobes onto the beds. It was exhilarating and somehow relieved the pain of losing our possessions.

WHAT I LEARNED FROM BEING POOR

I learned many important lessons during those difficult years. Most of all, I learned that poverty brings consequences that reach into every area of life.

I'll never forget the time the principal of my school called me into his office because I was not wearing the approved school uniform. He reached into his drawer and pulled out the thick wooden cane every student feared.

"How many times have I told you, you can't come to school dressed that way?" he demanded.

He didn't know that I had on my best clothes. I held up my hand hoping he'd give me a chance to explain, but he didn't. He ordered me to bend over and grab my ankles, and then he whacked me hard across my rear end—once, twice, three times.

"I'm sick and tired of your rebellious, obstinate attitude," he said when he'd finished.

My family had done a good job of keeping up appearances, so nobody knew what we were going through and I didn't want anyone to know. But the unfairness and humiliation of this caning was more than I could handle. Fighting back tears of pain and shame, I told the principal that my parents were too poor to buy me the required uniform.

His face turned beet red. He realised this was the truth, and he was terribly embarrassed over what he'd done. Although he never apologised, he took me to the school lost-and-found and helped me find an unclaimed blazer that almost fit me. From that day forward, I wore it to school.

It is funny, I suppose, but because my family was so close, I don't look back on the hungry years as being unhappy years—far from it. We may not have had any food in the cupboard, or wardrobes full of clothes, but we played cricket and other games together and generally had a great time when we weren't thinking about how hungry we were.

THROUGH ANN'S EYES

When we first married and Peter talked about being poor, I had a hard time relating. I grew up very protected and even attended a prestigious private school. I lived in one home from the day I was born until the day I got married. But Peter had lived through many experiences, many of them hard for him and his family. Those qualities became a part of who Peter is and the ministry we would one day begin.

Years later, after we started serving the Lord, I would also discover what it was like to give up the surety of a regular income. More importantly, I would hold the hands and bodies of those who were poor beyond my wildest imagination.

Poverty changes the ground rules, and it's been that way for thousands of years. Even the book of Proverbs states, "People do not despise a thief if he steals to satisfy himself when he is starving" (Proverbs 6:30).

Here are some of the key takeaways Peter has told me he had from those lean years. He discovered:

- The importance of sharing what you have with the

poor, even if you don't have very much at all.

- How to dream: Peter tells me he would fantasize for hours about being a successful soccer player and making enough money to build a better life for his mom and dad. This ability to dream, to see the big picture and plan for tomorrow, has served him well over the years.
- There is an excitement that comes from living on the edge, never knowing what tomorrow will bring. The safe, secure life can be stifling. Because of this revelation, later in his life, when God called Peter to step out in faith and take risks, he was ready to say, "Yes."
- Finally, the importance of family: Everything Peter and his parents went through, they went through *together*. They leaned on each other and made it through.

THE HOUSEKEEPER WHO LOVED US

It was also during this time that I discovered a truth that would shape who I became in years to come—a truth that was demonstrated to me through a gentle, caring black woman who came to work for my mother.

Sarah showed up one day and asked my mother if we needed a housekeeper.

Of course, Mom told her no—even though she was pretty sick at the time and needed help. We didn't have enough money for essentials like food and medicine. We certainly couldn't afford a housekeeper.

Sarah only laughed. "Oh, that's all right. You don't need to pay me. Don't you have a room where I can stay?"

As a matter of fact, we did. Like many other houses in Johannesburg at that time, ours had a room in the back that was built to house domestic helpers.

The woman persisted, so Mom made a deal with her. In exchange for allowing her to live in the room, she would spend one day a week cleaning the house and taking care of household chores.

As it turned out, she worked five days a week, and I loved it because, up until then, most of the housework had fallen on my shoulders!

My mother kept telling her, "You're doing too much. You know I can't pay you."

Sarah would laugh. "That's all right." Sarah was almost always laughing and smiling. "I enjoy the room."

Every few days, Sarah would walk to the shops and come home with a basket full of fresh vegetables for our table— tomatoes, carrots, squash, potatoes, peppers—all sorts of delicious things.

The first time she came in with a big basket, Mom eyed her suspiciously. "Where did you get all that?" But Sarah explained that she went around to the back of the fruit and vegetable store and dug through the trash to find vegetables that had been thrown out because they were no longer fresh.

That made sense, except the vegetables she brought us didn't look like discards. They were plump, firm and tasty.

One day about four or five months later, we heard a loud commotion coming from Sarah's quarters. Her boyfriend was shouting, Sarah was crying, and from the sound of it, things were about to get out of hand.

We rushed to her room, discovered that her boyfriend was yelling and hitting her, while she cowered on her bed, covering her head with her arms to protect herself.

My dad pulled her boyfriend off her and pushed him away. "What's going on here?" he demanded.

The boyfriend was livid. "She's been stealing my money! She's been doing it for months, and I just now caught her."

Dad turned to Sarah. "Is this true?"

Between sobs, Sarah admitted, "Yes, it's true."

This was how we'd gotten our fresh vegetables. Sarah, though she had next to nothing, hadn't stolen to buy for herself, but for us. Her heart broke when she saw how little we had to eat.

It was wrong that she had stolen money from her boyfriend, but even as a young man, I remember feeling so touched that she had gone to such great lengths to help us. As Dad led the boyfriend off our property, I couldn't take my eyes off Sarah.

This surprise moment became a pivotal event in my life because it turned my view of the world the right way up. My parents weren't racists or supporters of our government's apartheid policies—those policies that had segregated and discriminated against people simply because of the color of their skin. But I suppose that, growing up in South Africa, I couldn't help but develop a worldview that said . . .

- White people are "stronger" or "better" than black people.
- We were rich. They were poor.
- We were givers. They were takers.
- Assistance should go from whites to blacks, and not the other way around.

Sarah shattered those worldviews. From her, I learned that we're all in life together, regardless of culture, education or skin pigmentation. We need to help each other.

That value became part of who I am . . . and a principle I'd face later in life again and again as governments and workplace conditions challenged my new worldview.

Had that been the one lesson I'd learned from my early years, it would have been worth every sacrifice, but before things got better, they got worse.

"HE'S GOT A GUN!"

When I was about 15, events occurred that sent my life spiraling out of control.

On a clear, sunny morning, I sat at the school bus stop, minding my business, when, out of the corner of my eye, I saw a boy about my age approaching. I didn't pay much attention until he was almost beside me, and then—

WHAP! He kicked my shinbone.

"Hey!" I put my arms up to defend myself.

He tried to kick me again, but I jumped up and pushed him away. This time, he swung at me with his fist, but I ducked the blow and punched him in the mouth. Before he could react, I hit him again and again. Blood trickled from his nose and out of the corner of his mouth, but I wasn't through. He staggered backwards, and I knocked him to the sidewalk. I had never seen the boy before, and had no idea why he had attacked me, but I was determined that he would pay for this, and he did.

It wasn't until I got to school that I heard the news from a classmate. "Hey, you know that kid you beat up this morning?"

"Yeah?"

"He's in a gang. You'd better watch your step."

He was right. Over the next few weeks and months, I lived in constant misery. That boy was a member of a Lebanese gang that harassed me regularly. They waited outside my house and let it be known that they would beat me to a bloody pulp if they caught me. I was willing to take on any of them, one at a time, but not all of them at once.

Anytime I wanted to go out, I had to crawl out to the hedge surrounding our property to see if they were out there waiting for me. Most of the time, they would be, and I'd have to turn around and crawl right back into the house.

One night, I desperately wanted go to a party on the other side of town, so I slipped my father's pistol into my pocket for protection. I made it to the party just fine, but coming home, I wasn't so lucky. As I walked through a park late that night, I found myself face-to-face with 15–20 of my enemies.

"You're not so tough now, are you?" They surrounded me like a pack of wild dogs circling their prey. Some of them held clubs. In the moonlight, I saw the glint of a switchblade. One of them moved closer. "We're gonna kick your . . ."

I pulled my dad's gun out of my pocket and waved it around.

"He's got a gun!"

"Run!"

BLAM! BLAM! BLAM!

I have no idea how I managed to miss them all, but I'm grateful I did. I could have destroyed someone's life and spent the rest of mine in jail.

Not long after, I joined a gang myself and started carrying a chain and a knife. It was for protection. But soon I was involved in—and getting a kick out of—senseless violence. It gave me that adrenaline rush I loved.

Our idea of "sport" was going to the wealthy northern suburbs on a Saturday night, finding a house party to crash and beating up everyone there. We also destroyed as much property as we could. Even among the other members of my gang, I had a reputation for being hard and tough. I never ran from a fight. *Never.* If somebody got the better of me, I got even. I had no mercy.

I'll never know how I managed to survive—or stay out of jail. The only explanation is that even then, God had His hand on me. I'm also eternally grateful for the strong relationship with my father, which helped me through those difficult times. I could always count on my dad, and the power of his love undoubtedly saved me from going completely off the deep end and becoming a gangster forever.

THE SUEDE JACKET

In addition to being there for me, I knew I could count on my dad, no matter how tight things got, to provide for us.

For me, one of the most difficult aspects of being poor, was that I was at the age when every boy wants to look cool. And it was hard to look cool in patched jeans, or clothes purchased in second-hand shops and at rummage sales. Amongst my friends, all the cool guys wore suede jackets, and I really wanted one.

I knew there was no way my parents could afford to buy a suede jacket. It was ridiculous for me to even think about it, but it didn't stop me from wanting one.

Imagine how surprised and delighted I was when my dad came home one day with the jacket I had yearned for. I felt like I was in heaven as I tried it on and studied my reflection in the bathroom mirror.

Dad wore a huge grin. "What do you think, Peter?"

"It's perfect, Dad. Thank you!"

My mother had an incredulous look on her face as I strutted around, feeling like that soccer star I'd always dreamed of being. I saw the look my mom gave my dad, and I knew what it meant: "Isak, where on earth did you get that jacket?"

She was probably afraid that he had stolen it, but he just winked at her as if to say, "It's all right."

I later learned that my dad had taken two of his expensive tailored suits, suits he'd bought when he was making a good income, and he'd sold them to get the money to buy my coveted jacket.

I don't think there's ever been anything in my life that meant more to me. That was my dad. He loved us, and he always did his best for us. He wasn't perfect, but maybe his actions helped me years later to accept my Heavenly Father as a provider too.

CHAPTER 3

THE HORRORS OF APARTHEID

JOHANNESBURG, SOUTH AFRICA, 1963–1977

Over the three years my father was out of work, the South African economy gradually improved. Finally, he was able to find work, and what a wonderful day that was for the entire family.

I knew immediately that I wanted to go with him, and work for him. I was still two years away from my high school diploma, but school bored me and I wanted out. As far as I was concerned, school was a complete waste of time. I didn't believe I was learning anything that would prepare me for life. I wasn't learning anything that would help me make money or acquire assets or property. The only thing I liked about school were the sports, but I'd finally decided that it was time to give up the dream of becoming a professional athlete. Even gang life had lost its luster.

I dropped out of school, married my childhood sweetheart at the tender age of 17 years old and within three years had two adorable sons, Wade and Kevin, born in 1963 and 1966 respectively. I worked as a truck driver for my dad, even though when I started, I wasn't yet old enough to get a driver's license. Every time I passed a policeman on the road, I was afraid he would pull me over. It all went fine until one day when I couldn't stop fast enough and plowed into the back of the car in front of me.

Realising that I was only about a mile from home, I jumped out of the truck and took off running. I called my dad from a public phone, "Dad, I've been in an accident."

I told him where it was, and he jumped in his car and drove out to the accident scene. By that time the police arrived, they assumed he had been driving.

Despite a few setbacks like these, my father saw that I was hard working and a quick learner. By the time I was 22 years old, I was the site manager of all our building sites. My dad ran the company, but I ran all the jobs.

It was about this time that I realised I needed education in business, so, although it meant I would have little time at home, I went to night school and earned a two-year diploma in business management and accounting.

Those were difficult years. It took a lot out of me. Classes were five nights a week, from 6 p.m.–10 p.m. each night. I almost never saw my wife and two sons. I managed on very little sleep as I worked 12–14 hours every day, and still needed time to study when I wasn't in class.

Somehow, I made it through, and my newfound knowledge quickly paid off.

Soon after graduation, Dad called me into his office. "I've been watching you and I'm convinced that you could do a better job of running this company than I can."

"But Dad . . . " I protested.

"Now hear me out," Dad sat back in his chair. "With my experience, I'm also convinced that I can do better at project managing our job sites."

"What are you suggesting? That we swap roles?"

"Exactly."

And so, at the tender age of 25, I took over as Chief Executive Officer of a rapidly growing construction company, employing more than 100 people. I wasn't sure I could do it and was amazed that my dad had so much faith in me. What if I made bad decisions and ran the company into the ground? I remembered those three terrible years my family had endured. Now we were back on top, and I was determined to keep us there.

Within three years, the company tripled in size. We made tremendous money. We had come a long way from those days of not being able to afford school uniforms, of not having any running water in the house, of taking appetite suppressants so we wouldn't feel the pain of hunger. It was a season of prosperity.

"Could life get any better than this?" I would soon learn the answer to that question.

HATING THE SYSTEM

During the mid 1970s, we worked in five of the black townships surrounding the city of Johannesburg. Insurance companies hired us to to rebuild structures that had burned to the ground during anti-government riots. Most of our work involved the rebuilding of government buildings and community halls. I took comfort in knowing that we worked for the insurance companies, not the government. I had seen enough of the government's racist policies to know I would never agree to be on the state's payroll.

These were lucrative jobs because the situation wasn't safe. Riots often raged around us while we worked. On more than one occasion, we saw police come in with guns blazing, shooting down up to 20 people. Sadly, the police never thought twice about using deadly force. Then, at night on the TV news, we would hear an altered report of what had happened. Instead of the 10–20 people who had died, the media would report that only one or two people had been killed in a riot. Obviously, the government controlled what the media reported. White residents of South Africa did not know the truth of what was taking place in the black townships.

We saw unarmed people beaten into unconsciousness by groups of policemen with clubs. Vicious police dogs attacked others. It made me sick to my stomach.

The more I worked among black people, and saw their struggles, the more I hated the system that robbed them of their dignity and kept them powerless and poor. I saw the conditions they lived in, and I felt horrified. My heart often thought back to Sarah, our housekeeper, and the lesson she had taught me. We were all the same . . . we *needed* each other . . . so how could my country behave in this way?

One way the government kept these people down was by requiring them to obtain a permit to work in a white area. Of course, that permit was virtually impossible to get. None of that mattered to me. I saw no reason to comply with the policies of a government I hated, and I knew what it was like to desperately need work. So I hired them.

Many times, the police invaded our worksites, and those 'illegals' feared for their lives. I saw how terrified they were, how they would climb over walls, do anything they could to get away when the police arrived. One day, a man fell off a roof and suffered permanent injuries, just because he was trying to get away from the police.

And yet, there were times when riots raged, and we could have been targeted, simply because we were white, yet our black friends surrounded and protected us. They could have hated us because of the color of our skin, but they didn't. They knew we were their friends, and that we cared about them, even though we were constructing or repairing buildings that represented the government they hated.

THERE HAS TO BE MORE

Our business earned plenty of money, but for me, it didn't offer much in the way of excitement. I was now working sixteen hours a day and just like during my years in business school, I once again rarely saw my wife or children. I didn't want to spend the rest of my life working this hard. There had to be more.

So even though I didn't know a thing about farming, I left the construction business and began making my living from the land. To my wife's and my delight, in 1974, our third child, a beautiful little girl who we named Tania, was born.

My daddy-heart melted each time I held her. Unfortunately, our time on the farm didn't last long. Our marriage failed, and we all returned to the city of Johannesburg.

Divorces are always difficult, and mine was no exception. My heart ached for my children. Fortunately, within a short space of time, I was awarded custody of both Wade and Kevin.

I returned to construction, and although I could generate a good income from it, something inside me was empty. I battled with an overload of work and painful stomach ulcers. A part of my heart was still back on that farm and my dreams kept leading me there.

FALLING IN LOVE

Back in the big city, after a time of disillusionment and loneliness, I met Ann, a skinny, freckle-faced divorcee with a cute 18-month-old son, Grant. I fell in love. Within a few years, when I was 31, Ann proposed to me, and we married. We believed we loved one another enough to face and overcome the challenge of building one cohesive, happy family from a group of emotionally hurt individuals. No challenge looked too hard for us, if we could only live life together.

Wade, a meticulous perfectionist, top scholar and sportsman, dreamed of being a pilot, something that had once been a dream of my own. Kevin, just three years younger, enjoyed social activities and sports, with a host of friends who constantly surrounded him. To him, boring school classes were a waste of valuable playtime. I could relate. Tania, born 11 years later, remained with her mother and visited us only during school holidays. I loved every moment we were together.

We all enjoyed a lot of fun family times as we got to know and better understand one another. But what I really wanted was to move away from the city and begin farming. I discussed it with Ann, and with her and our family's agreement, we sold our construction business and moved to the Eastern Lowveld of South Africa, to take up the challenge of farm life.

THROUGH ANN'S EYES

I had grown up protected and safe, then married young at 20 years old . . . only to discover 18 months later that the dreams I had imagined were completely unrealistic. It was life-shattering. I had a beautiful little boy, but my life was empty, and I was suddenly alone. I felt like I was living in shock. Then . . . Peter.

We met because we had some of the same social circles and business connections. For a while, we both felt a bit disillusioned by relationships and wondered if we were really in love, but we both felt gracefully *safe*. Neither of us yet knew Jesus, and we looked for a solution to our loneliness. Peter had three children, and I had one. At 24 years old, I believed we loved each other enough to take on the world.

EVERYTHING ACCORDING TO PLAN

Ann was expecting our baby, so we worked out the best timing for our move, considering school changes and all that goes with the relocation of a ready-made family. On 6 May 1977, it was a new and wonderful experience for me to attend the birth of our son. I was so proud of Ann who had struggled through a difficult delivery. By her choice, and to the delight of my parents, we gave him my dad's name, Isak. Little did we know that he would be a child who would bring us so much joy and laughter, just like his Biblical namesake. Isak was a calm, contented baby who fit in with our busy schedules. Soon after his birth, we made the move.

With the money we made from the sale of our business, we bought two adjoining farms. On one, we would grow tobacco; on the other, we would sell the sugar quota and plant pecan nut trees. The land was beautiful with over 500 acres of gently rolling grasslands and sandy loam soil, with a mile and a half of river frontage on the Crocodile River. Numerous large flat-topped Lowveld thorn trees grew in the valleys, surrounded by a beautiful range of mountains and covered with thick, pine forests.

As we were close to Kruger National Park, where indigenous wildlife runs free, it was sure to be a wonderful place to raise our blended family. Perhaps this was truly what life was all about—being in harmony with nature and working the soil with our hands.

Within three years, our farms thrived and we even won the tobacco growers' "Golden Leaf Award" for the highest yield. After some rough years, it now seemed that, like King Midas, everything I put my hand to turned to gold.

Life on the farm was wonderful—just what I had been looking for. It had a calming influence on me and made the troubles of my youth seem far away. It was hard work, but I loved it, and living in the country suited us. My dad spent as much of his time as he could helping us as he loved farming. I felt even closer to him as we could relate to each other equally as adults rather than as father and child.

This new lifestyle greatly assisted us as we worked to build one strong, united family, refusing to use the word "step" in our reference to one another, "in case we trip over the step."

If all went as I planned, I figured we could retire comfortably by the time I was 40 years old. I felt that this was what I'd been looking for all my life.

But I couldn't have been more wrong.

A few years later, following my father's heart attack and miraculous recovery, my cousin Jannie would ask me if I was ready to serve Jesus. It was a loaded question that would keep me up all night as I considered where I'd come from . . . and where I was about to go. But soon it would become clear that what I was looking for was Jesus, and God had plans for me.

CHAPTER 4

GIVING MY LIFE TO JESUS

THE TOBACCO FARM,
EASTERN LOWVELD, SOUTH AFRICA, 1979

I couldn't stand it anymore.

At 5:30 a.m., after a night of restlessness, I knocked on Jannie's door.

"I want to give my life to Jesus. I know I can't go any further without Him."

Jannie embraced me, we both knelt and he led me in a prayer.

Nothing had ever come close to giving me the feeling that I had the minute I asked Jesus to come into my life. I was suddenly alive in the way I had always wanted to be.

I knew that from that day, 13 December 1979, my life had a new purpose.

Everything I had tried—joining a gang, zipping around a race track at 160 miles per hour, piloting my plane, risking great sums of money on the turn of a card, running my own successful business—all of that suddenly seemed dull and boring when compared to the excitement of a personal relationship with the Creator of the universe!

END OF MY DAREDEVIL DAYS

I knew that our lives had changed forever. Ann and I would never again be content with the way things had been.

Strangely, I no longer felt any urgency about rushing out to my tobacco barns. I knew I had tens of thousands of dollars' worth of tobacco curing in those barns and it needed my attention. During the curing process, tobacco must be checked every three hours to make sure the humidity and temperature are at the correct levels. The slightest variation will cause the leaves to rot, leading to financial disaster.

Suddenly, I didn't care all that much. I had discovered something else that was more important than making a living. Instead of going right to work, I went into town and bought Bibles for almost everyone we knew. I had never been inside a Christian bookstore before, and all the wonderful things I discovered amazed me. I spent hours browsing, feeling like a hungry kid in a bakery. I wanted to devour it all.

By the time I got home, with my car full of Bibles, it was nearly 4 p.m. And still, I ignored the barns. Instead, Ann and I sat in our living room, selecting a Scripture to write in the front of each Bible as we prepared to mail them to those we loved. We didn't know anything about the Bible, but somehow, we found a verse that seemed appropriate for each person. Joy and excitement filled our hearts, and we wanted to share it.

My heart overflowed with love for God, and a new love for my wife and family. Everything had changed. Nothing seemed impossible any more. Everything looked brighter. The air I breathed seemed to be infused with God's love. I was aware of His presence in all I did.

As I went about my work on the farm, seeing the sun set in the west and the moon rise in the night sky, an incredible rush of exhilaration hit me. I now knew the One who created the earth, the sun, the moon and the stars, and everything else I could see. And to think that He loved me so much that He was willing to send His Son to die for me! I wanted to laugh and cry and shout out loud for joy all at the same time.

Tobacco never entered my thoughts. Getting those Bibles into the hands of our family and friends seemed by far the most important thing we could do. When I finally returned to my barns, more than 24 hours had passed. I still felt like I was walking on air but as I approached the first barn, an unsettled feeling crept up inside me. How much of the crop had been destroyed? There would certainly be a great deal of damage.

To my amazement, everything was fine. *Everything.* None of the leaves had begun to rot. In barn after barn, I found the same situation. Tears welled up in my eyes as I realised that God must have taken care of things. There was no other way to explain it.

After that I knew my daredevil days had finally come to an end, but my days of defying death had only begun.

PART II

A VISION BEGINS

"If anyone desires to come after Me, let him deny himself, and take up his cross daily, and follow Me."

LUKE 9:23

CHAPTER 5

THE CALL

THE TOBACCO FARM, EASTERN LOWVELD, SOUTH AFRICA, 1979–1980

It was only a few months after I made Jesus the Lord of my life that I heard Him speak to me. It was unlike anything I had heard before, but I knew it was undeniably, unmistakably Him.

He simply said, *I want you to work for Me.*

"But what do You want me to do?"

I want you to preach the Gospel all over Africa and in the rest of the world. He went on to say that I would live out Mark 16. *I want you to understand that tens and even hundreds of thousands of people will receive Me through your preaching, even in one day. The blind will see, the crippled will walk and the dead will be raised to life again.*

I was taken aback. What an amazing thought! He would speak to hundreds of thousands of people through *me?* But could it be true? Could God use an ordinary man like me to do something this extraordinary?

Somehow, I knew He could. For in the days that followed that early morning prayer with Jannie, the miraculous began to happen.

WELCOME TO THE TOBACCO CHURCH

The first two weeks after I accepted the Lord were the most exciting of my life. I carried my Bible with me and spent as much time as I could reading it. The words seemed to leap off the page and into my heart.

At the end of each day, I couldn't wait to share with Ann the exciting things I had discovered. I found she experienced the same thing. When he left, Jannie encouraged us to find and attend a church in our town. The first one we tried was a Pentecostal church. We found the people somewhat strange, but they seemed to be so happy that we returned the next Sunday and the next.

Then, in the third week, I felt an incredible passion in my heart to tell others about what God had done for us. I figured that the best place to start would be with the 142 labourers who worked on our tobacco farm. Every morning before work, we met for roll call, and I announced, "This coming Sunday, we're going to have church here." I didn't tell them that I would be the preacher. Or that I'd only been to church a few times.

We got to work stacking the bales of tobacco onto one side, making space in one of our barns where we could hold "church" on Sunday afternoon.

When the day of our first service came, Ann and I went to church that morning. I paid careful attention to what the pastor said and took careful notes. I'm sure he thought I was a good listener. He didn't know I intended to preach the same sermon on my farm a few hours later!

I wasn't as polished as our well-trained, seminary-educated pastor, but what I lacked in eloquence, I made up for in passion.

All our workers arrived. Some sat on the ground. Others perched on bales of tobacco. When I looked out at the sea of beautiful faces, I felt overwhelmed by how much Jesus loved those precious people. They had worn their "Sunday best," most of which were ill-fitting, baggy trousers. Some had jackets that were so big they hung from the shoulders and were folded back several times at the cuffs. At one time that had also been my Sunday best. I knew from personal experience that clothing doesn't make the person.

I had always tried to treat my workers fairly, and made sure they received an honest day's pay for an honest day's work. But now I saw them differently, not as truck drivers, tractor drivers, skilled or unskilled labourers, but as people for whom Jesus had died.

Many had huge families. Sadly, throughout Africa, parents had come to expect that some of their children will die from illness or diseases from contaminated drinking water. A couple may have eight children, figuring that four of them may hopefully survive to adulthood. The ones that do survive will take care of their parents in their old age. Having many children is Africa's social security.

The workers listened intently to my sermon, and when I gave them an opportunity to pray and invite Jesus to be in charge of their lives, a few came forward and I prayed with them.

Ann and I were thrilled!

For the next three weeks, we followed the same routine. We attended the church service in the morning, I took copious notes, and then nervously smoked a cigarette on the way back to the farm where I preached the same message in our afternoon barn service.

I'm sure that ours was one of the strangest smelling churches ever. The place reeked of tobacco. And, for all my enthusiasm, I was not a powerful speaker. I sometimes stammered and stuttered, and I couldn't always read my notes. Nevertheless, within the first three weeks, 40 of our employees received Christ.

I realised what God could do through anyone who is willing and available to Him. I found a verse in Romans 12:11, "Not lagging in diligence, fervent in spirit, serving the Lord." We didn't have much in the way of education or training, but we had plenty of zeal and a fervent spirit, and God used it. We knew nothing about church structure or tradition, but because of that, we were free to allow Jesus to do whatever He wanted to do in our services. There was nobody saying, "But we've never done it like that before."

We were like children in our understanding. Later, we were happy to find the scripture which says, "unless you change and become like little children, you will never enter the kingdom of heaven" (Matthew 18:3, NIV). That was us: spiritual children with a desire to follow God.

"PLEASE DON'T LET HIM DIE!"

A few days before our sixth Sunday service, I came across exciting verses in Mark 16. As soon as I read them, I hurried to tell Ann, "Did you know Jesus said we can lay our hands on sick people and they'll get well?"

"Really?"

"Yes, it's right here." She looked over my shoulder while I read Mark 16:18: "'They will lay hands on the sick, and they will recover.'"

"So what are you going to do?" Ann asked, although I'm sure she already knew. On a farm with more than 140 employees, someone was always sick.

"I'm going to start praying for the sick this Sunday, just like Jannie prayed for Dad."

"Are you certain?" Ann searched my eyes. "Don't you have to be a registered preacher or something?"

"I've read it over and over," I told her. "I even went back and re-read the fourteenth and fifteenth chapters to see if I was missing something. Verse 17 states, 'These signs will follow those who believe.'"

She agreed I was right.

"I believe that means that what is written here will work," I said, "even through me."

With Sunday a few days away, I had time to prepare. I didn't want someone to ask for prayer, and then stand there while I tried to figure out where to place my hands. I finally decided that it would be best to put my hands on the person's shoulders, and to ask for healing "in the name of Jesus."

That Sunday, toward the close of the service, I read the passage in Mark 16 again and then said, "If you are sick, I want you to come forward so I can pray for you." No one moved. Then, slowly, five men rose to their feet and made their way to the front.

The first to reach me was a frail-looking old man who walked with a slight limp. I reached out and put my hands on his shoulders. "In the name of Jesus. . ."

WHAM! Before I could say another word, he crumpled backwards to the ground, like a bolt of lightning had struck him.

The others in line stepped back but didn't seem to be terribly concerned. Most of them had a strong belief in the supernatural world and did not find it surprising that God could cause a man to fall to the ground. Ann and I, on the other hand, had no clue what had just happened. We felt the temperature begin to rise.

Ann, who had worked for a time as a dental nurse, knelt down and checked the man's pulse. His heartbeat was strong and his breathing seemed fine.

I motioned for help from some strong men nearby. "He needs some fresh air." We carried him outside and placed him in the shade of a Maroela tree. I removed my jacket and fanned the fellow in a desperate attempt to revive him. "Jesus, I wanted for him to be healed," I prayed. "Please don't let him die."

Ann continued to check the man's pulse.

I asked, "What do you think is wrong with him?"

She shook her head. "I have no idea, but his pulse is strong and he seems ok."

After a few minutes, the old man began to stir.

"Thank you, Jesus!" I said under my breath.

Suddenly, he sat straight up with a big smile on his face. He wanted to go back inside.

"No! You can't go back inside," I told him. "You're an old man."

I reasoned that he had probably fainted from heat exhaustion, and that the best thing to do was to wrap up the service with a short prayer, so that's what we did. After that, for the next three Sundays, I insisted that the "victim" of my prayer should not be allowed into our church but that he should sit near the door, so he could get fresh air.

And I didn't say another word about praying for the sick. I was too afraid to do so.

COULD IT BE THE DEVIL?

My fears were made worse when I talked to an elder at the church we attended.

"You'd better be careful," he told me. "The devil can do strange things sometimes."

The devil? But how could the devil be involved when the desire of our hearts was to heal someone from sickness *and* the Bible said it was possible?

Even though I was afraid, a passage from Mark 16 kept running through my mind: "And these signs will follow those who believe . . . they will lay hands on the sick, and they will recover." I thought of those words when I laid down at night, and they came back to me first thing in the morning. It was as if God was challenging me to believe Him and His Word, and to respond in obedience.

"But, God," I argued, "You saw what happened the last time I tried to pray for the sick. I was afraid that old fellow was going to die."

But there was no arguing my way out of it. I eventually gave in. The very next Sunday morning, I announced that anyone who wanted to be healed should come forward for prayer. To my surprise, no one hesitated. A dozen or more men and women came forward seeking healing.

I put my hands on the shoulders of the first in the line and asked for healing "in the name of Jesus." Almost as soon as I touched him, he collapsed to the ground. But this time, I didn't stop. I prayed for the second in line, and she fell. So did several others as I prayed for them. In my younger days, I had seen people fall down, but only after I had hit them as hard as I could! These people I was merely touching . . . gently and with love, and the power of God struck them down. It *had* to be God. There was no other explanation.

GOD'S AUDIBLE VOICE

As time went on, everything seemed perfect for Ann and me. We should have known what that meant: change was in the air.

Both of our farms were successful. Our house was full of beautiful, healthy children that we adored. Most of our employees now had a relationship with Jesus, and it felt to us like we were more of a family than a business. I had found the personal peace and satisfaction I'd searched for during my younger years and figured my life would be pretty much perfect from now on.

Boy, was I wrong! Everything was about to change, including me.

It had been a little over two months since I had come to a relationship with Jesus, and I could tell that I was becoming a better husband, father and employer. Yet I wasn't exactly living the "perfect" Christian life.

For one thing, I smoked nearly four packs of cigarettes a day and sprinkled my conversation with swear words. I didn't realise that my behaviour might be offensive to God or that He wanted me to clean up my act. I suppose I thought that if He was working through me, He must be happy with me. I didn't know that God would use anybody who believes and is available to Him. Although we had seen many supernatural healings and other manifestations of God's power in our little church, I was not prepared for what He was about to do.

It happened on a Wednesday morning as I was heading out to work. A lit cigarette dangled from my lips as I went into the farmhouse kitchen to pick up my thermos full of coffee. Suddenly, I felt light-headed and dizzy. Then I heard a voice: *Stop smoking and get baptised.*

That was all. I didn't look around to see who had said it, because I knew beyond any doubt that God had spoken to me. I felt like a child who'd been caught misbehaving by his father. Panicked, I reached up, grabbed the cigarette out of my mouth, smashed it in my hand and let it fall to the floor behind my back, as if I thought I could fool God into thinking that I hadn't been smoking.

THROUGH ANN'S EYES

I'll never forget that moment, a few minutes later, when I walked into the kitchen to get a cup of coffee. There stood Peter, and as soon as I saw the look on his face, I knew something amazing had happened.

"God spoke to me," he said.

That was news. "He did? What did He say?"

"He told me to quit smoking and get baptised."

"That's wonderful!" I exclaimed. I had been after Peter for a while to quit smoking, and now I had a powerful ally!

I grabbed the telephone to call a friend from church.

"Guess what? God just spoke to Peter in my kitchen and told him to stop smoking. That's right! God spoke in *my* kitchen!"

GETTING MY ATTENTION

Ann was thrilled. But I'd had the biggest fright of my life. That's the only time God has ever spoken to me in an audible voice. I've had people say to me, "I wish God would speak to *me* that way." But that's not the way I see it. I figure He had to speak to me out loud because that was the only way He could get my attention.

I didn't light up another cigarette all day long. I was too afraid.

That night, Ann and I went to hear a visiting Bible teacher from the United States at the little church we'd been attending on Sundays. Before the service, we sought out the pastor because I wanted to tell him what had happened. Before I could say a word, he said, "Peter, we're having a baptism service this Sunday, and I wanted to speak to you about getting baptised."

"Yes," I said, "I need to get baptised."

Then imagine my surprise when the sermon started and the visiting speaker spoke on hearing God's voice! He explained that God speaks to you by a small inner voice, or giving you peace in the decisions you make, or by directing you to a passage in the Bible. Then he said, "And if you're so stubborn that you won't listen, He might even speak to you in an audible voice."

Ouch!

I was baptised the following Sunday.

A RAGING INNER BATTLE

Nonetheless, a battle raged inside me as I struggled to obey God with regard to not smoking. More times than I can count, I reached for a cigarette and then found the strength not to light up. It was like there were two people inside of me engaged in an ongoing and, at times, violent battle:

Come on. You can have a cigarette. It's not like God isn't going to forgive you.

Oh, no. You aren't going to disobey God. There's no way that is going to happen.

For three months, the battle raged. It nearly drove me crazy. My craving was made worse because I worked around tobacco all day long. Then, mercifully, my desire to smoke went away and never returned. I haven't smoked another cigarette since that day when God told me to stop. That's the impact God's voice can have on a person.

Smoking won't keep someone from getting into heaven, but

it's an addiction that had a strong hold on me. When God told me to stop smoking, I knew I'd been given an opportunity to prove to Him, and to myself, that I was serious about living this new life. With God's help, I would succeed. It was the first of many difficult things God asked, or rather commanded, me to do. And I've done my best to obey.

In the wake of my obedience however, it seemed like all hell had broken loose, with one incident after another that was trying to kill me.

"I THINK HE'S DEAD!"

The first of those happened on a Saturday after I had spent the morning working in our tobacco barns. I always came home for lunch by noon, but on this day, I became distracted and forgot the time. When I didn't show up as promised, Ann sent our then 16-year-old son Kevin to find me.

He hopped onto his 125cc off-road motorbike and headed to the barns.

Meanwhile, I realised the time and rushed home on my little Agri farm bike.

The grass was tall, and the road curved. We were both riding in the middle of the road, heading straight toward each other. I came around a curve and—

"Look out!"

We slammed head-on into each other at around 35 miles per hour, flying in opposite directions.

One handlebar cut Kevin's leg, but he was not seriously injured otherwise. He hobbled over to where I lay on the side of the road. Neither one of us had been wearing a helmet. Kevin feared the worst as he looked at my crumpled body.

One of our neighbour's farm workers saw the crash and me lying motionless on the ground. She ran all the way to our house, banged on the door, and yelled for Ann to come quickly.

Ann threw the door open. "What's going on? What's wrong?"

"It's Peter," the woman explained. "He's been in a terrible accident. I think he's dead!"

I was still alive, but only by the grace of God. I kept passing out en route to the hospital and my whole body hurt. The doctor in the emergency room explained that my knee had taken the full force of the impact when I was thrown from my motorbike. It was a miracle that my entire kneecap hadn't shattered. I was bleeding badly and, amongst my other injuries, the tip of my little finger had been sheared off and the nail ripped out.

The doctor stitched me up as best as he could and sent me home, ordering me to take it easy for at least a week. Even though the pain in my knee was intense and my hand was immobilised, there was no way I could obey those orders. Farming is a demanding career, and within a couple of days, I resumed work.

But it wasn't over yet.

INCREASING THE HEAT

While I was still recuperating from these injuries, I discovered that my employees had not stoked one furnace properly so the barn temperature wasn't as hot as it needed to be to cure the tobacco. Realising that this could cause a catastrophic loss to our tobacco crop, I stormed over to the barns to take care of it.

I was angry, thinking to myself, "If you want to get something done right, you have to do it yourself." I grabbed the solid iron poker, which was about nine feet long and poked the fire in the furnace to get the heat to increase.

"Okay, that ought to do it," I thought.

I pulled the poker out of the fire and leaned it up against the wall, alongside a water pipe. The bottom third of it glowed from the intense heat, having just come out of the furnace.

As I turned to go, I heard a noise behind me. I turned around and saw the poker falling over the water pipe and the red-hot end of it bounce up right between my legs.

"No!" Instinctively, I grabbed it with my hands and closed my legs. "Aaarrggghhh!!!" The pain was excruciating.

Somehow, I managed to hobble out of the barn, and Ann drove me to the hospital. I'd been wearing shorts that day, so I had two long, third-degree burns up the side of each leg, and across both my hands.

This time, I stayed in bed for two days, right in the middle of tobacco-curing season, because of those burns. I continued to trust God and never once considered turning my back on Him.

But it *still* wasn't over.

A TRIP TO THE WITCH DOCTOR

As I lay in bed recovering from my injuries, I heard a tremendous commotion coming from the barns. People were shouting and yelling, and I thought I heard a wild dog barking. I threw on some clothes and hobbled out to see what was going on.

On my way, two young men ran past me, their eyes wide with fright, racing as fast as their legs could carry them in the opposite direction.

"What is going on?" I called out. "What are you running from?"

They acted as if they didn't hear me, so I picked up my pace, although I still wasn't moving very fast. As I got closer to the commotion, I could see about 25–30 people running around as if playing a crazy game. But it wasn't a game. They attempted to catch some kind of animal. Or, rather, some kind of animal attempted to catch them.

People shouted and danced out of the way as the ferocious beast lunged and snapped at them. I could hear it growling and barking, and I wondered why somebody hadn't caught and killed it. The people who worked on my farm weren't afraid of wild animals, and I couldn't understand why they were behaving like this.

Suddenly, the crowd formed a circle as one man tussled one-on-one with this rabid creature. I pushed my way through the circle and experienced a shock. One of my men struggled to keep a young woman pinned to the ground while she twisted and squirmed, barking like a dog and trying to bite him.

"What's going on?" I asked nobody in particular.

"She has a demon," someone said.

"A demon?"

She turned and glared at me, bearing her teeth and growling.

"Ow!" The man holding her lost his grip as she bit the back of his hand. She wriggled free and ran off into the nearby woods where she stood growling and barking at us from a safe distance.

I tried to convince everyone that she was harmless and urged them to get back to work, but they wouldn't hear of it. They wouldn't work as long as that woman was still around. They feared she would attack them at any moment.

"What can I do about it?" I asked.

"Take her to the witch doctor."

"The witch doctor?" They informed me that the nearest one was over 112 km (70 miles) away. It was the last thing I wanted to do, but they insisted, and if I refused, they would stand by and watch my tobacco crop rot.

I felt that I had no choice but to do what they wanted. It never occurred to me that this troubled woman could be set free from demons in the name of Jesus, but with my limited experience, it never crossed my mind. So with the help of some of the stronger men, I got her loaded into my truck and spent four hours driving her to consult with a witch doctor and then back home again. Of course, this costly venture didn't work. She still barked like a dog, although she did stop trying to bite people. We returned her to her family and, reluctantly, the workers agreed to get back to work, but we had already lost precious hours of harvesting.

By now I was completely exasperated. It seemed that ever since I'd tried to obey God, my life had been nothing but trouble. I felt like I'd been in the ring for a few rounds with a world heavyweight boxer. First, there'd been the motorbike collision, then the burns from the red-hot poker, and now we had a demon-possessed woman wreaking havoc on my farm.

To this day, it amuses me when I hear someone teach that life becomes a picnic once you accept Jesus. My experience has been the opposite. When God has a plan for our lives, a fierce battle rages. Yes, Jesus gives us victory as we trust Him and hold on in faith, but that doesn't mean we won't take a few nasty punches.

TAKING AUTHORITY

A few days after the incident with the demon-possessed woman, the pastor of a church in the nearby community of White River paid us a visit. He said he had heard about my burn injury and wanted to check to see if I was all right or needed anything. As he sat talking with us in our living room, he appeared uncomfortable, as if there was something he felt compelled to say, but didn't know how we'd respond.

Finally, he asked, "Do you mind if I say something?"

"Go ahead."

He was quiet for a moment as though searching for the right words. Then, "There seems to be an incredible, tangible spirit of fear in this place."

As soon as the words were out of his mouth, Ann burst out

crying. She told him everything we'd been through over the past few weeks, including the most-recent incident with the "dog-woman."

He nodded. "This is a spiritual attack. We need to take authority over it in the name of Jesus."

We knelt down right there in our living room, and he led us in a prayer, claiming the power of Jesus over the demonic forces that had warred against us. That day, we won a great victory over the overt powers of darkness.

THROUGH ANN'S EYES

Facing demonic forces and discovering the spiritual war going on around us was eye-opening. It was around that time that I discovered the power God had for us in the baptism of the Holy Spirit. It *empowered* us.

Not long after that, a local group invited me to speak at a women's Christian tea. I had no idea there were differences between people who called themselves Christians. I thought Methodists, Presbyterians and charismatics were all the same. One woman there was an ex-Catholic nun who had followed the Lord but still felt an emptiness in her heart. As I shared with her about the baptism in the Holy Ghost, I could see the lights go on.

However, sharing about the baptism of the Holy Spirit angered some of the women.

This baffled me. All Peter and I knew was that we needed God's power to do the impossible things He'd called us to do.

ACCEPTING THE CALL

When some find out we are in full-time Christian ministry, they say, "That must be the most wonderful thing in the world." Often it is, but it can also be the most difficult and dangerous work in the world.

As I soon discovered, Jesus meant it when He told His followers: "'If anyone desires to come after Me, let him deny himself, and take up his cross daily, and follow Me'" (Luke 9:23).

After God told me to quit smoking, I knew I had to give up the farm. It simply made sense. If my smoking displeased God, then I couldn't justify a living growing tobacco that enabled other people to smoke.

I still can't explain why, but even though I knew that God wanted me to get out of the tobacco business, I also knew that He had blessed my farm. I had lost several days of work to injuries and had endured a work stoppage due to the demon-possessed woman and yet we had more tobacco than ever. I could only assume that God's grace and mercy were present.

Although it was a tough decision, Ann and I sat down together and concluded that it would be our last year on the farm. After the crop had been sold, sometime in June, we would find something else to do with our lives, but we didn't know what.

Every day we prayed together about our situation, asking God to show us where He wanted us to go and what He wanted us to do. No answer came.

"Lord, can't you speak to me like you did about the smoking?"

But Heaven was silent, and June was only three months away.

Then late one night, as I was praying by myself in my study, I heard His voice. This time, rather than an audible voice, it was an inner conviction. I felt a rush of excitement and knew that it was from God.

I want you to work for Me, He said.

"But what do you want me to do?"

I can't remember if I said the words aloud, or just thought them, but His reply was immediate: *I want you to preach the Gospel all over Africa and in the rest of the world.* He continued, *I want you to understand that tens and even hundreds of thousands of people will receive Me through your preaching, even in one day. The blind will see, the crippled will walk and the dead will be raised to life again.*

Naturally, I was excited. I was also scared and confused. I couldn't believe God was saying those things to me, a baby Christian. I didn't know very much about the Bible, and I had grown up with no interest in the things of God. I suppose I acted the way Gideon did when God told him to rescue the children of Israel from the Midianites: "'O my Lord, how can I save Israel? Indeed my clan *is* the weakest in Manasseh, and I *am* the least in my father's house'" (Judges 6:15).

I felt like saying, "God, are You sure You've got the right guy?" All I wanted to do was make it through the tobacco season. As I thought about all the reasons why I could never be a preacher, travelling all over Africa and the world telling people about Jesus, I opened my Bible. I turned to the book of Revelation.

"And they sang a new song, saying:
'You are worthy to take the scroll,
And to open its seals;
For You were slain,
And have redeemed us to God by Your blood
Out of every tribe and tongue and people and nation,
And have made us kings and priests to our God;
And we shall reign on the earth'" (Revelation 5:9-10).

As I read those words, it was like a jolt of electricity passed through me. I saw that my past didn't matter to God. He would not hold it against me that I'd been a rebellious teenager, because the blood of Jesus had washed all my sins away. I was one of those "out of every tribe and tongue and people and nation" who He had redeemed.

Still, this seemed incredible. "Lord, how are you going to do this?" I asked. "And when?"

Again, I heard His gentle voice in my spirit. *When the time is right, I will tell you.*

I sensed that our conversation was over. There was nothing left for me to do but to wait on His timing. After all, He was in charge.

I walked down the hall to our bedroom, where Ann lay asleep. I sat on the bed for a moment, listened to her breathing and wondered if she was dreaming. My eyes filled with tears of love and gratitude. "Thank you, Lord," I whispered. "Thank You for my wonderful wife."

I moved to wake her and share what God had just told me,

but fear stopped me. What if she didn't think I had heard from God? What if she thought my imagination was getting the better of me? I didn't believe I could be obedient to God's call on my life if Ann wasn't in agreement.

Yet this burned in me, and I couldn't keep it to myself. I placed my hand on her shoulder. "Darling, can you wake up? I have something to tell you."

She stirred.

"Ann, wake up."

Her eyes blinked open and she sat up. "What is it?" She sensed the urgency in my voice.

"God just spoke to me."

"He did? What did He say?"

I took a deep breath and told her everything. I felt a twinge of embarrassment when I got to the part about the blind seeing, the crippled walking and the dead being raised to life again. It sounded over the top, but it was what I had heard, so I carefully repeated it.

When I finished, Ann said, "This is wonderful! I've been waiting almost two weeks for you to tell me that God has called you to work for Him."

I was astounded. "You've been waiting? But why? What . . .?"

"Two weeks ago, as I was driving on the freeway, I saw a flash picture of you behind a pulpit and felt God showing me that you will be a preacher and work full-time for Him. I laughed at the thought of it and felt I should wait until you became aware of this and brought it to my attention. It certainly wasn't a dream of mine!"

I took her into my arms, and we rejoiced in what God had planned for us, and we accepted His call. We still didn't know exactly what would happen or how God would do it, but we knew this would be the last year we earned our living as tobacco farmers.

There was one important question though: How were we going to repay all the money we had borrowed to develop the farm? We'd taken out huge loans to install the irrigation system, construct a dam and buy tractors and other equipment.

We prayed and asked God to help us become debt-free so we could begin working for Him right away.

THROUGH ANN'S EYES

When I was young, my parents exposed me to various religions. On Sunday morning, they dropped us off at Sunday School, but never joined us. They believed it was up to each individual to make their own decision about what they believed. Religion was about duty, never about a personal relationship with Jesus. Having known only a few religious formalities from the nuns at the Anglican church school I attended, I was in no way prepared for an understanding that God had called us. Yet, the desire to please Him and serve others grew stronger and stronger in my heart.

I knew that Peter was a man who constantly rose to the challenge of growing and learning new things. I had seen how well he had mastered the skills of effective tobacco production, a somewhat complicated practise that requires dedication.

Was the plan that God had for our future going to satisfy him or would his restless nature draw him into other distractions?

I often used to tell him that he was "an adrenaline junkie", saying that all he ever wanted was excitement, excitement and more excitement!

Little did I know what lay ahead for us and just how much we would need to know—beyond any doubt—that God had called us into this work.

BELIEVING BEHIND BARS

Wanting to preach was a strong desire in me, and I loved it. When the church we attended offered prison ministry, I jumped at the opportunity. When I arrived at the prison the first time, an officer led me down a cold, stone hallway into the dining hall. There, *hundreds* of prisoners sat. They turned to look at me when I walked in as if to say, "And who are *you?*"

If that wasn't daunting enough, my heart skipped a beat when I heard the doors to the dining room shut and lock behind me! There I was, a volunteer preacher packed in a room with some of the finest criminals South Africa had to offer. So, I did the only thing I knew to do. I preached.

And I preached.

And I preached.

And I preached.

For six months I preached, alternating weeks with another volunteer preacher. Not one person came to accept Jesus. Finally, one Sunday afternoon, I'd had it. I finished preaching, drove home, stormed into my study and threw my Bible down on the desk.

"Lord," I said, "Romans 1:16 says the Gospel 'is the power of God unto salvation.' I just want You to know, I'm not impressed with Your power. I've been preaching my heart out for six months, and not one person has gotten saved!"

Then, there it was, that voice speaking to my heart again. *Yes, you've been doing that. But when did you once go in believing that everyone would get saved?*

He was right of course. I hadn't believed for anything. I had done my best preaching, but I hadn't done my best *believing*.

"Lord, please give me one more try."

Two weeks later, after 14 days of pumping myself up with faith, believing and imagining that someone would respond and get saved, I entered the prison again and preached.

When the time came, I gave an altar call, asking anyone who wanted to make a decision to follow the Lord to come forward. To my absolute shock, more than 300 men got up out of their seats and came forward. I figured they must have misunderstood me, so I clarified what I was asking them to do. Another 30 came forward.

What happened over the coming weeks can only be described as a revival. These new prison believers wanted *more*. They wanted to be baptised. Without access to a pool, we baptised them in the prison showers—a high-speed sprinkling! Soon the entire prison was open to us. The officers told us that they used to dread coming into work, but something had changed. Now they arrived to hear hardened criminals *singing* praise songs. They said that the inmates were not misbehaving any more.

It was a miracle—and a milestone in my life. I learned a valuable lesson: If I wanted to see results in anything I did for the Lord from this point forward, I needed to start right. I needed to start with *faith,* specifically believing for a result, or I'd receive nothing. I needed to take God at His Word just as it was written.

IF WE CAN'T TRUST GOD, I'M OUT

We were soon to see that we served a God who regularly delights in performing miracles for His people.

In South Africa, a tobacco farm can produce two crops every year. The first crop is the big one and passes through the barns in November and December. The second crop is harvested a few months later and is generally only about one-third the size of the first crop, due to the cooler, rainy weather. Most farmers hope their second crop will provide enough money to care for and feed their staff through the winter months. There's not likely to be much excess. This is usually a time for keeping belts as tight as possible.

But this year, it was different.

Our second crop brought in six times more income than we expected. It far outsold the first crop and enabled us to pay off every cent of our debt. There was even enough money left over to sustain our family for an entire year! Ann and I both knew this could not have happened without God's intervention. There was no other explanation.

We figured that God would show us what He wanted us to do as soon as the crop was sold. We were anxious to go into full-time ministry, and we had told Him, "We want to start working for You right away."

I felt impressed to go to a small mission organisation in the nearby community of White River, where they printed Gospel tracts for distribution throughout Africa. I drove out the next day to volunteer. "Is there anything I can help you with?"

As a matter of fact, there was. They were desperately in need of new accommodations for their mission staff.

"I'll be happy to help you with that," I said. "I've worked in construction most of my life."

I admit that I was surprised, but I'm not sure why. By then I should have known that that was how God worked, bringing the right people together at the right time for the right purpose.

David Newington, the director of this mission, told me that they had already bought a small piece of ground where they had planned to build, so I went to look at it. I didn't like what I saw. A small stream of water ran the full length of the property with no easy outlet. The entire piece of land was waterlogged. I knew we would need to dig canals to drain the property before any building could commence.

When I reported this, Newington asked me to write up an estimate as to how much it would cost so they could take it to the bank to apply for a loan.

I was incredulous. "Get a loan? Why on earth would you want to do something like that?"

He had a blank look on his face, as if he didn't know what I was talking about. Looking back, I don't blame him. I was a young, enthusiastic Christian, filled with a desire to do things

God's way, but my zeal sometimes made me insensitive and, honestly, *stupid!*

I was talking to a man who had served God for many, many years and was known throughout Africa for his great adventures on the mission field. Who was I to flip out because he wanted to get a bank loan instead of trusting God for the money? But that's what I did.

"Count me out. If we can't trust God to provide the money to build this housing project, then I don't want any part of it."

I would not have blamed Newington if he had laughed at me, or told me politely that he would not need my services after all. But he didn't. Instead, he thought about it for a moment and then said, "Okay, you've challenged me. We'll do it your way."

"Great!"

Then he looked me squarely in the eye. "But I've got a challenge for you too."

I nodded, ready for anything.

"If that's how we're going to do it, then we'll both have to trust God every step of the way. Agreed?"

"Of course." That was exactly what I wanted to do.

"Good. Then let's start building."

I arranged with another farmer to make bricks on his land, which was ideally situated as it had a river running through it with perfect river sand for the bricks.

Everything was going along great until I hit the first obstacle. It had to do with my new car. After Ann and I had sold our final tobacco crop, we had enough money left to buy a four-wheel-drive Nissan, a car that I loved and had always wanted. We weren't too far into our brick-making project before I realised that we would need a truck to deliver the bricks to the building site. When I explained this to Newington, he said, "Well, you and I agreed that we would trust the Lord together. I'm trusting Him to provide money for the cement and bricks. I think this must be your part. You trust Him for the truck."

That wasn't what I wanted to hear. As I drove home that evening, I asked God, "How am I going to trust You for this truck? Where is the money going to come from?"

After dinner, I checked the newspaper classifieds to see if there were any trucks for sale. There were two that would suit our purposes. One was ridiculously expensive. The other seemed like a good deal, but it was still more than I had (which was nothing). Despite that, I called the phone number listed and got all the pertinent information. There was no doubt about it; it was just what we needed.

Finally, the man asked, "Are you interested?"

"Yes," I said, "I'm interested. But there's one little problem. I have no money."

"What?" He sounded angry. "Then why are you wasting my time?"

"I do have something I could trade. It is a new Nissan four-wheel drive."

To my surprise, he didn't hang up on me.

"Believe it or not," he said, "I was going to use the money from the sale of my truck to buy a blue Nissan four-wheel drive. What colour is yours?"

"Blue." I couldn't believe it. It was like a punch to the stomach.

"No, Lord", I thought. "Not my 4x4!"

I told the guy I'd have to call him back, and I hung up the phone. I knew what I was supposed to do, but didn't think I could bring myself to do it. "Please, Lord," I whined. "I've only had my Nissan a little over two months. Surely You have another way." But it was no use negotiating. God had made a way. "Yes, Lord." I had to trust Him.

It wasn't easy to pick up the telephone and call the fellow back. I told him I was ready to make a trade.

The man lived in Johannesburg, a four-hour drive from the farm. The next day, I set out on the road. The entire drive there, I kept remembering the story from Genesis, where God told Abraham to go into the wilderness and sacrifice his only son, Isaac. Not until Abraham put Isaac on the altar, did God instruct him not to harm the boy. "For now I know that you fear God, since you have not withheld your son, your only *son,* from Me" (Genesis 22:12). Then He provided a ram for the sacrifice. I wasn't equating my 4x4 with someone's only son, but I *did* love my Nissan!

I half expected that when I got to Johannesburg, God would show me another way to get the truck we needed. At least, I hoped He would. But it didn't happen. The man took my nearly new Nissan and gave me his truck. I drove home with a heavy heart. I suppose that if I had known at the time that God was about to ask me to give up everything, letting go of that Nissan wouldn't have been such a big deal. But at the time, it seemed very big indeed.

Of course, that truck turned out to be exactly what we needed, and a vital part of our building project. Seven months later, we completed our construction of the mission housing, without a single cent in loans.

WHERE TO NEXT?

By September 1980, Ann and I had grown close to David Newington. We told him we planned to sell our farms and move to the United States to attend Bible school. He felt strongly that this was not what God wanted for us. "I feel that you should get some experience in the local church, and then make your decision later."

Ann and I talked it over and believed this was the right decision, so we did as our dear friend advised. We entered full-time ministry.

CHAPTER 6

HOLDING NOTHING BACK

EASTERN LOWVELD, SOUTH AFRICA, 1980–1982

We were already involved in a small, local church, but we prayed that God would use us to a greater degree, and He did. We were both amazed when, only a few weeks later, David Newington came to us and said he wanted us to serve as associate pastors.

"We don't normally ordain people this quickly," he explained. "But we feel that this is what God is telling us to do."

We felt honored, but I let them know that the Lord had spoken to me and my true calling was to travel and preach the Gospel as an evangelist. They said they understood that we may only be there for a season. And so, only nine months after accepting Jesus into our lives—starting with the building of mission housing and now to pastoring the church—we entered into full-time ministry. Before long, with the tobacco farm sold, we moved into a small railway house near the church so we could serve however best the Lord could use us.

The church's leadership immediately put us in charge of the Sunday evening service. It wasn't as big of a job as we thought. Most of the folks in the church didn't even seem to know a

Sunday evening service existed. If twelve people showed up, it was a pretty good crowd. Usually it was under ten people, including Ann and myself. That didn't matter. All I wanted to do was preach and release the fire that burned in my bones. I also started praying for the sick every Sunday evening, and God responded with miraculous healings.

Word spread quickly. It wasn't long before the Sunday evening service attracted more people than the Sunday morning service! Both services grew as more and more people became saved, healed and filled with the Holy Spirit. Within six months, our Sunday morning service had grown from 85 to around 200 in attendance. Not long after that, both services were averaging more than 300 each week.

We even needed to expand the size of the sanctuary. God had blessed the church and I thought things were wonderful. I had no idea that some didn't agree.

I was shocked when, at one of our regular meetings, an elder told me, "Peter, we've decided that you must stop praying for the sick at our Sunday evening services." At first, I wasn't sure I had heard him right. But when I looked around the room and saw the stern looks on the others' faces, I knew they had all agreed on the decision.

"Why? Have I done something wrong?"

"No, we just want to make sure that everything we do here brings glory to God—and not to any man." The implication was obvious.

"I would never intentionally do anything to bring glory to myself," I replied. "I try to make it clear that God is the one who heals, not me."

"Yes, but we feel that some of the people may be looking to you, rather than to God."

I felt hurt and embarrassed, but these men were my spiritual leaders and I needed to submit to their authority. When I insisted that I felt that it was important to pray for the sick, the elders came up with a compromise. I could continue to invite those who were sick to come forward for prayer, and I could anoint them with oil. But the elders would do the praying. That was fine with me, so that's what we did.

To this day, I don't know why, but the healings stopped. People were sick when they came for prayer, and sick when they left. Disappointed and frustrated, I searched the Bible for confirmation of the elders' decision. I only found what God had laid on my heart, where Jesus had said, "'And whatever you ask in My name, that I will do, that the Father may be glorified in the Son. If you ask anything in My name, I will do *it*'" (John 14:13–14).

Bringing glory to the Father had certainly been my intention. I'd never been under the illusion that there was anything special about me. I knew that only Jesus had the power to work such miracles.

I felt somewhat like I imagined the Apostle Peter did, when the people were astounded after he healed a crippled man. He said, "'Men of Israel, why do you marvel at this? Or why look so intently at us, as though by our own power or godliness we had made this man walk? The God of Abraham, Isaac, and Jacob, the God of our fathers, glorified His Servant

Jesus . . .'" (Acts 3:12–13).

Although I didn't understand, I felt I had to stay submitted to those God had placed in authority over me.

CALLED TO MEET THE ELDERS

In the meantime, Ann and I had begun visiting the local hospital to pray for the patients there. It was a special place for us because a hospital was where it had all begun. I couldn't help but walk through the doors and be reminded of rushing to the hospital to see my dad on what I thought would be his deathbed . . . only to experience his miraculous healing, an experience that started us down this course.

Ann, in particular, saw amazing healings. When word got out, the elders called us in for another meeting. We were both shocked when they said, "We don't want you going to the hospital by yourselves anymore."

"I don't understand," I admitted. "Why wouldn't you want us to share God's love by praying for people who are sick and in pain?"

"Oh, it's not that. We just want to do it as a group."

We were bewildered. We knew God had called us into ministry. Why were we receiving so much opposition from fellow believers? Still, we both felt that God had called us to submit, so that's what we did. It was not easy.

Finally, after an entire year of situations like that, I felt it was time to talk with the leadership of the church and remind them that God had called me to be an evangelist. They assured me that they remembered my evangelistic calling, but the church needed me. The timing wasn't right, they said.

Before I knew it, another nine months passed, and I again felt compelled to remind the elders that God wanted me out on the road preaching the Gospel.

Again, they were reluctant to let me go, but that was about to change.

Over the next few weeks, people at the church treated us differently. They weren't as friendly as usual. Some acted as if we'd done something wrong, and we didn't have a clue what it was. It all came out at the next elders' meeting when one of the men confronted me.

"How could you do this to us?" he challenged me.

"Do what?" I asked. "I don't know what you mean."

He looked at me as if he didn't believe me. "We've heard all about it. How you're going to leave and start your own church."

I couldn't believe my ears. I had no intention of starting a church. When Ann and I left, it would be to go on the road for Jesus. Someone had evidently started a rumour that I was going to start a "rival" congregation, and it had spread through the church like a prairie fire. It almost seemed that Ann and I were the only two who hadn't heard it!

Of course, we were hurt. I asked, "When you heard this rumour, why didn't you come and ask me if it was true?"

It saddened us to find out that people we cared about had been talking about us behind our backs, and that they thought we were up to something underhanded.

As we shared our hurt feelings with God, we felt it was time to move on and start holding Gospel outreach meetings throughout the eastern side of South Africa. I was to preach the Gospel, lay hands on the sick and pray for their healing. It's what I was called to do.

EVERYTHING? REALLY?

In 1982, during my prayer time, I felt God prompt me that He wanted to use our nest egg of savings. I questioned the thought. "Lord? Do you really mean *everything*?"

I couldn't believe that God was calling me to be poor again. All those childhood memories of poverty came flooding back—the hunger, the humiliation, the desperation in my father's eyes, my mother's tears.

I had vowed that I would never be poor again. My children would never go to bed hungry or be short of their basic needs. No stealing milk or water or electricity or being embarrassed by their clothes. I'd worked hard to make that dream a reality, and I had succeeded. After selling the farms, we were set for life.

Our bank account provided us with the security we needed to launch into full-time evangelism. In fact, in all the time we had worked with the local church, we had never received a salary. God had blessed us so that we were able to give our time without taking the church's money. We had enough in the bank that we would never need to ask for anything. We were free to go anywhere God wanted us to go and to do anything He wanted us to do. Because we weren't depending on anyone else's support, we'd be completely free to follow God's leading in all things.

Surely, He could understand that . . . but He evidently didn't see things the way I did.

I wanted to obey God, but I never thought He would ask something like this of me. Had I not proven myself faithful when I gave up my cigarettes, my farm, my beautiful new Nissan? Why was God asking me for more? Then I told Ann what God had said.

"Are you certain you heard Him correctly?"

"Yes."

I had spent several of my teenage years in abject poverty. Ann, however, had never been poor. We prayed and read the Word, hoping that God would change His mind, but He didn't. We read about the blessings in this life, for those who give up houses, farms and other assets for the sake of the Kingdom of God. We both knew God was requiring us to trust Him. We wanted to obey, but we agonised at the thought of doing it. We knew we would be miserable if we disobeyed, but it was difficult to give up everything we had worked so long and so hard for.

We finally decided that we would get away for a few days, so we could talk and pray about this decision. We picked a beautiful spot on the coast. Everywhere we looked, God reminded us of the wonder of His creation. The ocean sparkled like blue diamonds. The clear surf washed gently onto soft sand that felt warm and inviting beneath our bare feet. The sky glistened a deep azure blue. The days were warm and clear. The nights were cool and invigorating.

But we hardly noticed the beauty surrounding us. Instead,

we spent almost every waking moment contemplating, agonizing over and rehearsing the consequences of this decision. After three days, we were no closer to a decision.

On the morning of the fourth day, I arose early and wandered onto the beach. I climbed up on some rocks and looked out over the sea just as the sun began to rise above the horizon. It was a morning that made you feel good to be alive.

"Lord, help me," I prayed. "I want to serve You, but it's difficult to do what You've told me to do."

As I looked out at the sea, sun and sky He created, I heard Him say to my heart, *My son, if you will give Me everything you have, then everything I have is yours.*

Suddenly, every bit of fear and reluctance drained out of me. The decision that had seemed so difficult and impossible a few moments prior now seemed easy. For the first time, I saw it. In exchange for what amounted to a tiny sum of money by comparison, God was willing to give me *everything* He had! God wasn't being unfair at all. It was too good an offer to pass up.

As fast as I could, I ran back to the camper, the sand kicking out under my feet. I woke Ann and told her, "God just spoke to me, and He said that if we give Him everything, then everything He has is ours."

She smiled softly. Her eyes sparkled as she took in the reality of such an amazing promise. "We're never going to get a better deal than that," she said. "Let's do it."

We knelt together and prayed: "Lord, all we have is Yours. We give You everything we own."

Deep in our hearts, I think we still hoped that once we

symbolically gave everything to God, He would bless it and give it right back to us. But He didn't.

I have heard it taught that when it comes to money, God is concerned about our motivations and attitude more than anything else. It's okay to have money in the bank as long as our priorities are right and we acknowledge that everything we have comes from God. I believe that's true, and I would never tell anyone that God demanded that they give away all their assets, but that's what He asked of us.

And so, we began giving our life savings to His work. We had already given some of it to help complete the apartments for the mission station. Some went to help enlarge our local church building. Much of it went to other ministries and poor families in our area.

Our next move was to buy a large tent, sound equipment, lighting and other materials for the *Jesus Alive Ministries* evangelistic outreach that God had instructed us to begin.

The Bible teaches us that "God loves a cheerful giver" (2 Corinthians 9:7). It was wonderful to spend all that money with a cheerful attitude, and we spent every cent as God directed.

We trusted that God would take care of us. We simply didn't know how, so it was a shock when for the next three years, we went through financial hell.

THROUGH ANN'S EYES

There were many days when we sat down to meagre portions and lean meals. When one of our children tore a hole in a pair of pants or a shirt, I needed to patch it rather than replace it.

We stretched every note and coin as far as it could go.

Peter and I came from very different backgrounds. I am one of six children, raised in a beautiful, large family home in a wealthy, lush suburb of Johannesburg. In the old colonial way, five servants waited on us. One of them was a chauffeur who, in his fancy uniform and cap, drove us to our private school each day in a large winged Cadillac. A butler, in a white uniform, served our meals in the dining room and, at the ring of a bell, brought our after-dinner refreshment order into the living room. Tea was served in beautiful engraved silverware, at 11 a.m. and 4 p.m. each day. I seldom ventured into the kitchen. At age 10, after being trained in formal manners and etiquette, my siblings and I joined our parent's table for dinner each evening. All of us, five girls and one boy, attended private schools where we were tutored in excellent academics and social graces like elocution, good deportment and more.

By contrast, life with Peter was different, but that's what had attracted me to him in the first place. I loved his *joie de vivre* and excitement to extract the maximum out of life. I was happy to run alongside him in our new adventures, the first of which was learning to be the wife of a tobacco farmer, living away from the city lights and wonderful shopping areas; then, moving into a small railway house while we co-pastored in the local church, with three of our children sharing one bedroom; now, living on meagre portions as we established a new ministry and became dependent on offerings from others.

One of my greatest concerns was how we would provide for our six children. It took a lot just to feed, clothe and educate such a large family. One day, as I was praying about this, I saw a massive crowd of young people and knew God had shown me that there are thousands of families with children world-wide who are working for Him. In the light of this, couldn't God provide for our six children? Was that really so difficult for Him?

As time went on, we realised that we still had hard lessons to learn. It was not until several years later that I became aware that all we had been through was teaching us to trust God. After all, if we couldn't trust Him to put food on our table and provide clothes for our children, how could we trust Him in the death-defying situations that we would face as we headed out on this new road in total obedience to His call?

I recall how embarrassed I felt when a preacher came to visit us and talk about our ministry. Our daughter Jackie, who was only about two years old, had fallen asleep on the sofa. I had put a throw over the back of the sofa to cover the stuffing that was popping out. It was a cool evening and our visitor wanted to make sure our little girl was warm enough, so he started to remove the throw to cover Jackie with it. When he did so, he saw how worn the sofa was, and he quickly replaced the throw. He said nothing, but we could see his embarrassment. And we felt humiliated.

A few days later, we received a cheque in the mail from this kind gentleman, telling us to use his generous gift for anything we might need. We certainly could have used a new sofa, but we didn't *need* one. This money went straight into our ministry. God taught us many things, not the least of which was humility and the foolishness of placing one's value in material things that are here today, gone tomorrow.

We were content, knowing we were where God wanted us to be and we were developing a closer, personal relationship with Him. However, sometimes Peter was frustrated by our financial struggles. Like any husband and father, he wanted to provide a good life for his family.

He didn't mind doing without things he had enjoyed for so many years, but he struggled with seeing his family do without. He felt pressure knowing that I had never been through such financial struggles.

It was during this time that our oldest son, Wade, in his upright manner, confronted us, challenging us on what looked to him as a lack of responsibility. "Dad, do you realise that you are giving away our inheritance? And besides, how will you provide for my brothers and sisters?"

We came to realise that this was how the situation looked to him and to many of our family members who did not understand.

Paul's words in the book of Philippians both challenged and comforted us: "Not that I speak in regard to need, for I have learned in whatever state I am, to be content: I know how to be abased, and I know how to abound. Everywhere and in all things I have learned both to be full and to be hungry, both to abound and to suffer need. I can do all things through Christ who strengthens me" (Philippians 4:11–13).

". . . YOU NEED TO FIND
ANOTHER CHURCH HOME."

We certainly couldn't count on our money or our investments to save us. We also discovered, in a rather painful way, that we couldn't count on other people.

I went to our church and told the leadership that the time had come for us to set out "on the road" for Jesus. I thought they would launch us out with their blessing. I hoped they would stand behind us with prayer and encouragement as we set out to take the message of the Gospel to those who had not heard the Good News. I would have been delighted to hear that they would even consider providing financial support for our ministry.

They didn't do any of these things.

Instead, they explained that our denomination didn't have a "vision for mass evangelism." They didn't deny that God had called us into an evangelistic ministry, but "if you plan on doing this, you need to find another church home."

Ann and I loved those people as our own family, so it hurt like crazy to leave. Only much later did we realise if we had stayed, it would have hindered what God had planned for us. We took comfort in knowing that Jesus had suffered rejection from those He loved too. Jesus had said, "Take up your cross and follow me," and that was exactly what we planned to do, no matter the cost.

CHAPTER 7

"GO DO THE IMPOSSIBLE."

SABIE & NELSPRUIT, EASTERN LOWVELD, SOUTH AFRICA, 1983

"What if nobody shows up? What if I heard You wrong, Lord, and this isn't really what You wanted me to do?"

My heart pounded, and a lump formed in my throat. I paced back and forth backstage at the community hall. Our first meeting was about to begin.

It was June 1983 in the small town of Sabie in the Eastern Lowveld of South Africa. Over the previous few months, we had officially established *Jesus Alive Ministries* and were in the process of registering as a charitable organisation.

Now, on the eve of our first outreach, I wondered if the whole thing was going to die a quick death. Ann and I didn't know what we were doing. We did get some help though. We had hired a wonderful Christian brother onto our staff who had never done anything like this before. And our song leader, who I had the privilege and joy of leading to Christ, had just been released from prison. So we had that going for us.

I couldn't recall ever being this nervous; not when I was turning corners at 150 miles an hour; not when I took my first solo air flight; not when I had thousands of dollars riding on the turn of a card in a casino.

I looked at my watch. We were half an hour from start time. I wondered if anybody had arrived yet so I slowly made my way across the backstage, afraid of what I would find. I peeked through the break in the curtains, hoping that at least a few seats would be filled. What I saw shocked me. The auditorium was filled beyond capacity. Hundreds of people packed into the place. In fact, three people shared every two chairs.

I was thrilled so many people had come to hear about Jesus. And, I was terrified.

I ran back to my "prayer room" at the back of the stage and closed the door. "Lord, I can't do this! There are too many people here!"

That gentle, loving voice I had come to know so well resonated deep in my heart. *You may have never done this before, but I have done it many times. You can go out there and preach, and I will be with you.*

That's exactly what I did. I preached. And I still felt inadequate. I didn't feel that I was particularly eloquent, confident or powerful. As I looked out at that huge audience, I couldn't tell if my words were getting through or falling flat. However, when I invited all those who wanted to accept Jesus to come forward to the front of the hall, almost everyone in the audience responded. Not only did they respond, they couldn't wait to come down and surrender to the Lord. I learned that night that God's power is made perfect in our weakness, and that the success of *Jesus Alive Ministries* didn't depend on me or

Ann or anyone else. Our success depended upon God alone.

I still had many other important lessons to learn, one of which was to obey God in every situation. God had instructed me to pray for the sick every night at the end of the service. Once the people had returned to their seats after responding to the altar call, I invited any who needed special prayer to come forward so I could lay hands on them and pray for them, trusting God to answer their needs.

As I was ready to begin praying, out of the corner of my eye, I saw two men coming toward me, carrying a middle-aged woman. The men had joined their arms and crossed them to create a makeshift chair for her. The lady balanced in their arms, her legs dangling uselessly in front of her. They brought her to the front of the auditorium and helped her into a real chair. She was crippled like that invalid I'd seen as a youth at the Oral Roberts crusade. Almost completely helpless on her own, she needed a powerful touch from God.

I'm ashamed to say that my faith failed me.

I wasn't a famous evangelist. I reminded God that this was my *first night* as an evangelist. I told Him I wasn't ready to pray for someone who had such a monumental problem. Maybe after I'd been on the road for a while, I'd be ready to pray for the crippled, but not that night. I told Him it would be better if I stuck to illnesses no one could see, like colds and headaches.

And amid my doubt and fear, God reminded me I could trust Him. *Pray for that woman before you pray for anyone else.*

I ignored Him and prayed for others.

Pray for the crippled woman.

"Lord, I just can't." I continued to pray for those who were well enough to stand in a healing line. Again and again, God urged me to pray for the crippled woman who waited patiently with her two companions.

Finally, everyone *except* the crippled woman had received prayer and, frankly, I was relieved that it was over. Not one person showed signs of healing. I didn't ask anyone to testify of what God had done for them, because I wasn't sure anyone had experienced healing.

Anyone looking from the outside would have seen what I was doing and thought I'd been blessed with mountain-moving faith, but inside, I was just a man, or less . . . a quivering bowl of gelatin. I was like the man who asked Jesus to heal his son, and then, when the Lord spoke to him about faith, said, "'Lord, I believe; help my unbelief'" (Mark 9:24).

I headed back to the stage to close the meeting.

Are you going to disobey Me?

"Never, Lord."

You just did.

"What? How?"

I told you many times to pray for the crippled lady, and every time you have disobeyed Me.

I stopped in my tracks. It hadn't even crossed my mind that I was being disobedient by refusing to pray for the poor soul. I was so focused on my own feelings of inadequacy that I hadn't even realised that I'd disobeyed God's command. It was time to make things right.

"I'll pray for her right now."

I turned and walked down to where the lady sat. But even then, although I was going to pray for her, I didn't walk straight to her. I didn't want anyone in the audience to see what I was doing. That way, if nothing happened, I wouldn't be embarrassed, and they wouldn't be disappointed.

At the last minute, I took a few steps in her direction, put my hands on her head and said, "In the name of Jesus, be healed." That was it. Then, as quickly as I reached her, I moved on, heading back up the stairs and onto the stage. At least I had done it. I had finally obeyed.

Suddenly, commotion. I turned and saw the crippled woman had jumped out of her chair and was bouncing and twirling around the auditorium! Sheer joy filled her face. She was *dancing* on legs that had been paralyzed and useless just a few moments earlier!

The congregation cheered. Everyone was thrilled. But my heart was broken. I felt so ashamed that I had disobeyed God and that, because of that, I had almost denied that dear woman the healing miracle that God had for her.

I dismissed the gathering in prayer, then ran to the back room and fell face down. Tears flowed as I repented, realising that God had wanted to heal that woman before I prayed for anyone else, because it would have triggered so much faith in others. I *failed,* and it probably kept some people from receiving the healing they desperately needed.

As I wept, I felt God's love and encouragement assuring me that I would still see great things as I did what He told me to do.

The rest of that week was incredible. By the time we were ready to leave town, we had seen close to 2,000 people surrender to Jesus. We had also seen people filled with the Holy Spirit, healed of all sorts of illnesses and, at one point, we even saw the Holy Spirit fall like a cloud across the auditorium.

We returned home fired up and ready for our next outreach in Nelspruit. We expected to ride into that city on a tide of victory and power. We didn't know that we were about to go through a time of severe testing.

CAUGHT IN THE CROSSFIRE

In the early 1980s, the fight against apartheid tore South Africa apart. Ann and I had never believed in or supported our government's racist policies. From the very beginning of our Christian walk, our stand on racial issues was guided by Galatians 3:28: "There is neither Jew nor Greek, there is neither slave nor free, there is neither male nor female; for you are all one in Christ." This stance did not endear us to our government, and caused difficulty for us in the early days of our ministry.

In places like Nelspruit, we were at risk due to our opposition to apartheid. We didn't preach against the government's policies, but we showed by our actions that we disagreed with the notion that a man or woman with light-colored skin is superior to a person whose skin is dark. Plus, we held outreach meetings in black homeland areas and black townships. This alone was enough to make some people consider us enemies and traitors. And here I was invading our black brothers' and sisters' space, a white preacher with an Afrikaans name.

Over the ensuing years, being unwelcome would become a recurring theme. Our pro-apartheid government tried desperately to hang onto control. The country was torn by political violence, and atrocities were common on both sides. We would be threatened with arrest several times because it was illegal for white people to sleep in black areas. Police would even search our office more than once, and charge us with a lawsuit for running a 'multi-racial club' after one of our neighbours saw a black person swimming in our swimming pool.

In these difficult days for South Africa, Nelspruit, in particular, was a city divided by political hatred, violence and crime. The day before the outreach began, as we set up, I heard what sounded like a firecracker, only much louder, going off. I looked in the direction of the noise and watched in horror as a uniformed policeman, gun in hand, ran my way. There was another popping sound, and something whizzed by, just over my head.

"Down!" I shouted. "Everyone down!"

"Lord, protect us," I prayed. "We came here to serve You. Please don't let anyone be killed."

We hugged the ground as bullets shot back and forth above our heads. The shooting continued for only a few moments, but it seemed like hours. Finally, it stopped. I lifted my head and looked around, grateful for the silence. Shaking, I rose to my feet and checked on everyone. No one had been injured.

It turned out that an armed robbery had taken place across the street from the hall where our outreach was to be held. Of course, the experience frightened us and reminded me that I had a wife and six children who depended on me. After all the wonderful things I experienced in Sabie, I once again wondered if I was doing the right thing.

If I said that was the last time I would ever ask that question, I'd be lying. I have discovered that stepping out in faith to fulfill God's calling brings challenges. I've also discovered that it's necessary to hang in there, knowing that God is always there to help fulfill His calling.

For our Nelspruit outreach, we had rented a hall that seated 2,500 people. Many of the local citizens were suspicious of outsiders—including *us*. The first night, at least three-fourths of the seats remained empty. What made it worse was that the few people who attended at all sat in the back of the hall. It was as if the people kept us at arm's length, wanting to hear what we had to say, but not wanting to get involved. Several times, I asked people to come forward and fill the seats toward the front, but they refused.

As I stood on the stage, preaching to a sea of empty seats, I could feel an attitude of anger and rebellion permeating the atmosphere. It seemed like everyone was against us. Amid all this hatred and violence, we knew there was only one way to bring a peaceful transformation to our beloved country— through the love of Christ. It alone was the only antidote for the anger and strife that divided our people. Still, the message of love that I preached didn't seem to penetrate in Nelspruit. I finished my sermon and gave a fervent altar call, pleading with those who were lost and brokenhearted to come forward and experience the grace and mercy of Jesus.

No one stirred.

I gestured to the row of local pastors who sat in folding chairs behind me on the stage. "We're all here waiting. We would love to pray for you," I urged.

Everyone stayed glued to their seats; 500 pairs of eyes stared at me without the slightest hint of emotion.

A REPEAT PERFORMANCE

The second night was a repeat performance.

Attendance increased, but once again, the front half of the hall remained empty. And, again, not a single soul came forward to receive Jesus.

When the same thing happened on the third night, I was beyond frustrated. Frankly, I was angry that people would turn their backs on the opportunity to accept salvation.

"Jesus loves you," I pleaded. "He's here tonight, and wants to save you. Please come forward so we can pray with you to receive Him into your heart."

Still nothing.

I remembered how Jesus had told His apostles to shake the dust off their feet in a city that wouldn't receive them (see Luke 10:10–11). I wondered if that's what we should do—pack up and go home.

Then, to my surprise, two women slipped out of their seats. They slowly walked to the front of the auditorium. Sometimes, a flood begins with a small trickle. I hoped the courage of these two women would spark a response from others who had wrestled with coming forward themselves.

As I moved to pray with those two women, the power of God hit them like a thunderbolt. The power of God lifted these women off their feet and threw them backward onto the ground. They landed on the tiled floor with such force that the sound echoed throughout the hall.

The auditorium became deathly quiet. The two of them lay on the floor motionless. I half wondered if they were dead. My heart raced. "God, I didn't do this. You did." I could see it: first they blame us, then a riot ensues.

Then one of the women rolled over onto her knees and sobbed. I couldn't understand what she said in her own African language, but she clearly poured her heart out to God loud enough for everyone to hear.

Then the other woman moved onto her knees too, weeping and crying.

Later I found out that both of these women confessed their sins before God and everyone else. It was the spark everyone needed. People throughout the auditorium rushed to the front, many crying and shouting their confessions as they came. For the next 20 minutes, people wept before God, as His love and grace washed over them, setting them free from their sins and the spirit of rebellion that had bound them. What had started out as one of the most frustrating experiences had become a memorable night of miracles and healing.

To dismiss the meeting, I handed the microphone to a local pastor to lead us in a closing prayer. He took the microphone, bowed his head and opened his mouth to pray. Before he could utter a single word, the power of God hit him and he flew backward, disappearing through the stage curtain. He landed flat on his back with only his legs sticking out! The divine presence of God had certainly demonstrated His awesome power.

The next day, word of what had happened spread throughout the community. That night, every seat was full—and this time, there was no hanging out in the back. People packed the place from wall to wall. The people of Nelspruit's township had given up their rebellion against God.

By the time we left town, Ann and I had both learned that things don't always start well, and they don't always work out the way we want them to. However, if we persevere, God will come through. We have reminded one another of this truth over the years as obeying God's Word has often put us in one dangerous and difficult situation after another.

A STEP IN THE WRONG DIRECTION

It seemed that we were always "walking on the water," being challenged to believe God for money to pay for each month's expenses. How I longed for a bit of wiggle room in our bank account. It would have been wonderful to at least have enough money set aside so that we didn't need to worry about every last detail of our budget for a couple of months.

That's when I made one of my biggest mistakes ever. My intentions were pure, but it nearly dropped us into a hole we couldn't climb out of.

It all started when I attended a workshop hosted by a Christian organisation on how to raise funds for missionary work in Africa. The speaker talked about how the Apostle Paul had supported himself by making tents.

"We shouldn't be afraid to use our hands to supply our needs," he said.

It sounded good to me and, in fact, it still does. It just wasn't the solution God had in mind at that time for our ministry, and I had not received confirmation from the scriptures that this was part of His plan for us.

I came home excited about the possibility of using my skills in building construction to support our mission. I decided that I would build an entire subdivision of townhouses. I put an excellent business plan together, took it to the bank and received approval for a loan although I had no collateral to offer.

What happened next was much like what had happened to my father in the sixties. Just as the townhouses were ready for sale, the political situation in South Africa deteriorated and the economy followed. I had dozens of beautiful homes to sell and nobody to buy them. It was like I was thrust back into a shadow of what we had faced when I was thirteen. I could feel the grip of poverty clutching at my throat.

It would have been bad enough if I had used my own money to build the houses. Instead, we were now deeply indebted to the bank on top of everything else. We faced a substantial, immediate payment and had no way to make it. If we defaulted on our loan, the bank was sure to sue us, and that would bank-rupt us and, by extension, our entire ministry.

Ann and I spent our weekends trying to sell the town-houses, doing all we could to advertise them and get them sold to no avail. I tossed and turned through many sleepless nights, berating myself over what I had done. Repeatedly, I asked myself how I could have put our ministry on the line this way.

I paced back and forth, wearing out the carpet at 3 a.m., trying to figure out a solution. There seemed to be no way out. Night after night, I ended up on my knees in anguish. "Lord, I am so sorry that I made this mistake. I have brought our whole ministry into disrepute. What will I do if they sue me?"

How many times are you going to repent for this thing? I heard the Lord ask me. *I heard you the first time you said you are sorry. It's time to stand up and trust Me. I am ready to deliver you out of your problems.*

I looked forward to seeing exactly how He was going to make *that* happen.

"WHAT SHOULD I DO?"

It would have been wonderful if God had told me where there was buried treasure or if He had opened the skies and rained down money from heaven. Instead, I felt Him compelling me to ask every one of my creditors not to sue.

That didn't sound like much of a plan, but I felt certain it was the *right* thing to do. I would promise to pay them and even though I had no idea where I would get the money, I felt sure God would provide.

As far as I knew, not one of my creditors was a believer. They were businessmen who focused on the bottom line. I didn't think the "please don't sue me because God will provide" strategy would go over well.

But I also knew better than to disobey.

I went to my biggest creditor first. That influential man had already threatened me with a lawsuit. Standing in his office, I forced my voice past the lump in my throat as I asked him not to sue me. I promised that I would repay every cent.

He reacted as predicted. "And where are you going to get the money?"

My heart pounded wildly as I looked him in the eye. "God is going to give it to me."

He was quiet for a moment. Then, to my surprise, he nodded and said, "Fine. You have six months."

The story repeated itself everywhere I went. Not one of my creditors laughed at me or turned me away. And, as happens when one obeys, the funds showed up just when we needed them.

CHAPTER 8

TRAGEDIES THAT EMBOLDENED US

BUSHBUCKRIDGE & SHATALE, LIMPOPO LOWVELD, SOUTH AFRICA, 1983

Our ministry outreaches continued and God provided. The crowds became larger and suitable town halls became harder to come by. We decided we needed a large tent that we could take on the road. We found one at a good price that would seat close to 5,000 people. The manufacturer advised us that they would send a man from Johannesburg with the tent, and he would teach us all about maintenance, transportation and more.

Delighted with our new tent, we soon set out for an outreach in Bushbuckridge. Watching us try to set up that tent would have given any onlooker a good laugh. We looked like parents trying to assemble their children's toys on Christmas Day. It took us ten times longer than it should have. With the participation and amusement of some of our children, we took turns swinging large mallets at tent pegs, pounding them into the sun-burnt, hardened African soil.

The tent was huge, and it did not seem to want to cooperate as each gust of wind billowed under the tent fabric, moving it in another direction. Thankfully, we were able to get everything up and ready to go in time for the opening night, and 5,000 people came out to hear the Gospel. But then the unexpected happened, and I almost lost all of them.

LOST IN TRANSLATION

Some teenagers sitting in the front were moving around, laughing and whispering to each other as teenagers often do. As they disturbed others, I looked at them and said, "Please, if you are going to stay in the meeting, sit down and behave. And if you can't behave, then please leave."

Almost immediately, most of the audience stood up and walked out en masse. There I was, standing on the stage, looking out at only 200 of the remaining people. All I could think of was how Jesus must have felt when His apostles deserted Him on the night of His betrayal. I looked over at my interpreter to see how he was reacting, and he merely smiled at me as if nothing was wrong.

"What in the world is going on?"

I had no idea what to do. Should I close the meeting and tell the rest to go home or should I continue with my sermon? I decided to keep preaching. After a few minutes, everyone who had left came back into the tent and took their seats. It wasn't until the service was over that, thanks to one of the local pastors, I found out what had happened.

"I don't think you understood what your interpreter said when you told those young people to behave themselves."

"What did he say?"

"He said, 'If anyone needs to take a 10-minute break, now

is the time to do it."

Talk about something being lost in translation!

Despite such amusing and, at the time, stressful moments, the Bushbuckridge outreach was where our ministry really caught fire. Night after night, God demonstrated the truth of His Word with signs and wonders. Blind eyes opened, crippled people jumped out of wheelchairs and tumors disappeared before our eyes.

I had almost forgotten the trouble we had encountered in Nelspruit, and now it seemed like nothing could stop us.

"THEY'RE GOING TO KILL YOU."

We then travelled to a place called Shatale.

The first two nights were terrific. Again, God moved with tremendous power, bringing salvation, healings and other miracles. On the third night, the local pastors who assisted us came to me and said they felt it would be best if we closed the outreach.

"What? Why would you want to shut it down? Everything is going so well."

The pastors looked at each other, as if they didn't want to tell me what was going on, but I insisted.

"Well, you see," one of the men said, "we have a gang in this city."

Another man nodded. "We always do what they say. We have no choice."

I had been in a gang once. I knew this could be serious business. "Go on."

"They said that if you continue to preach, they are going to come here and kill you."

"Kill me? But surely. . ."

"This is not an idle threat. We think it would be best if you left town now."

DO ANGELS WATCH OVER US?

A part of me wanted to turn around and run. Not that I was afraid to die. I had never been afraid of danger, but the thought of leaving Ann and our children was more than I could bear. We had poured every cent of our savings into this ministry, and I wondered how she would get by without me. Then I remembered that her life was in God's hands, just as mine was.

The local pastors' downcast eyes reflected their concern for my well-being. I was aware of their fear. Nonetheless, I could not do as they suggested and leave town. I felt strongly that we should continue to preach the Gospel and all would be well.

The following night, as the service was about to begin, I noticed something unusual. The tent was packed, as always, but the back row was empty. When I asked if anyone knew why, I got a chilling answer. The gang that had threatened to kill me planned on being in the audience that night. They had put out the word that the back row was to be reserved for them, and clearly, their word was law.

As I was about to preach, they walked in. There were 25 of them. Although they were young, it was evident that they had seen many battles. They were frightening, and the leader, who led them into the tent, looked the most menacing of them all.

Nobody dared turn to look at them. The fear they inspired was palpable.

I felt calm knowing that God was on my side, and I sensed His anointing as I preached. The members of the gang sat quietly, listening to what I had to say. I knew they could rush the stage at any minute and try to stab me, or pull out a gun and shoot me, yet I couldn't let that stop us.

Strangely enough, they didn't heckle me or try to disrupt the meeting. Most of them sat there with their arms crossed, angry scowls etched across their faces. I reached the end of my sermon and, as always, asked all who wanted to surrender to Jesus to come forward. To my great surprise, the big, tough, mean-looking leader of the gang was the first one out of his seat.

"Here he comes," I thought. "This is it for me."

Instinctively, I took a couple of steps backward, figuring that there was no reason for me to stand there and make myself an easy target. That's when I noticed the tears streaming down this man's face. He had come to kill me, but God's love had changed this hater's heart.

His sincerity was clear as he repeated the prayer of salvation. "Jesus, I acknowledge that You died on the cross for me, and I ask You to forgive me for my sins. Come and be in charge of my life from this day, and give me a new life." A joyful smile replaced his angry stare. The transformation was astounding.

Sadly, his conversion did not come without a great price. That night, as he left the tent, his own gang members attacked him. Angry over what they saw as his betrayal, they stabbed him numerous times, and he was admitted into the hospital in a serious condition. Thank God that he recovered, and, rather than seeking vengeance, sought out his attackers to tell them what Jesus' love had done for him. Eventually, he started a ministry of his own, and former members of his gang made up most of his ministry team.

To this day, it gives me chills when I think about that moment. Not because someone planned to kill me, but because God brought all the pieces together and thousands of people came to Him as a result. I will be forever grateful that I didn't close our outreach when I first heard about the threat on my life.

THE HAMMERMAN

Despite God's protection from the gang members, the fear of violence persisted. After all, this was South Africa—a country in turmoil. Bloodshed was common, especially hostility sparked by racial hatred. Thousands of white families left South Africa during these years, resettling in Australia, New Zealand, Canada, England and other English-speaking countries where they felt safe.

Oppressed and brutalised for centuries, many South African blacks determined to throw off their chains by any means possible. Yet as bad as it was, much of the murders, beatings and violence never made it onto the censored media.

It was during this time that a series of particularly brutal murders broke out in the Empangeni area of Natal, a peaceful town near the coast in Zululand. The killer randomly chose his victims, broke into their homes at night and murdered them in their sleep by smashing their skulls with a hammer. He was dubbed the "Hammerman." People in that community were scared as they realised that the murderer was still at large. A columnist in *The Observer,* wrote:

> Perhaps he's already decided where he will strike next. It's as if the darkness and insecurity is filtering in through our very windows . . . The fear has become an infectious disease . . . it grows and intensifies in the hours of the night, and yet it gets us nowhere. When fear of the Hammerman recedes, a new fear will take its place. Every new day will bring new fears, because we don't know, and not to know is almost always to fear.

THROUGH ANN'S EYES

My youngest sister, Terri, was living in Empangeni with her husband Jay, their two-year-old daughter, Lee-Ann, and four-year-old son, Shane. Terri and Jay were all too aware of these murders, so when a suspicious-looking man who seemed to match the wanted posters showed up at their trading store—"a man with eyes like fire"—they called the police.

Unfortunately, he was gone by the time the police arrived. His disappearance certainly didn't leave Jay and Terri feeling secure. That night Jay went to bed with a .32 revolver beside the bed.

But it didn't help.

Not long after this, Jay's friend, Dave, who lived with them, arrived home in the early hours of the morning, and found the most horrifying carnage awaiting him. The Hammerman had entered their home and bludgeoned both Jay and Terri to death. Remarkably, the killer had not harmed the children, even though evidence showed he had visited the children's bedroom. Investigators thought he might have tracked them to their home because they had identified him and reported it to the police.

As soon as I heard this horrific news, I felt an overwhelming need to pray and, as I did, I was astounded by my own words: "Father, forgive him, he didn't know what he was doing." I instantly became aware of the forces of evil that had driven this man to commit those awful murders. As I prayed, I sensed the hatred, anger, malice and unforgiveness wanting to enter my being, but stronger still was a strong "river of forgiveness" flowing out of me, hindering the entrance of those negative and destructive feelings. Despite that heinous crime, how could I harbor hatred in my heart?

My second prayer was to ask God to apprehend this man before he could attack again.

Three days later authorities arrested the Hammerman, Simon, in the sugar cane lands. During his trial, he told the heart-wrenching details of his life. Malan, a Rian police journalist and author of the book, *My Traitor's Heart*, recorded the story:

> *The Hammerman's real name was Simon Mpungose. It was apparent that there were many others who shared in the guilt of what he had done. The murders*

he committed were the work of one man. But in many ways, they were the fruit of his tribal ideals combined with a repressive, racist system that made it extremely difficult for someone like Simon to succeed in life.

It turned out that Simon's mother died when he was a young boy and due to certain tribal assumptions, even his relatives didn't want him and made that known through regular beatings and other cruelty. In his teens, he was arrested for stealing, and sent to prison. He tried to tell the judge that he only stole because he was hungry—that long days of backbreaking labour did not bring him enough money to stave off starvation. It made no difference.

In prison, he had made the first of several suicide attempts, trying to hang himself with a frayed piece of rope. But the rope snapped, and he sprawled to the concrete floor of his cell, bruised but otherwise unhurt.

Over the next few years, Simon was in and out of trouble with the law—mostly for theft. He was finally sentenced and sent to a prison in Barberton, South Africa.

I won't go into all the details of what Simon experienced in that prison, but the evidence presented during his trial included guards beating him so severely that he could not walk for a month. Other prisoners were beaten to death in front of him because they had dared to 'talk back' to the warden.

Simon spent his days working in the prison quarry, breaking rocks with a hammer. He eventually began to imagine that the rocks he was smashing were white men's heads.

It was during this terrible time that Simon had what he thought was a prophetic dream, in which he saw himself killing a faceless, white tormentor with a hammer. "And when I had killed him, they took me away . . . and they put me to death and I had freedom from torment."

As many Zulus would, Simon believed the dream was a message from his ancestors, a revelation of his destiny. When the time finally came for him to be released from prison, he asked the commandant to help him get a job in one of the Johannesburg gold mines. There, he would live and work with other blacks, and would not have contact with whites. Thus, there was no way his dream could come true. Although he did not give his reason for wanting to do so, he also said he was willing to stay in prison if that meant he would not be sent home.

The commandant laughed at him and told him he was crazy. He was given fifteen rand (less than US $3), provided with a few items of clothing, and put on the train for his hometown of Empangeni.

There, he again found himself unable to make a living. For months he had to endure prejudiced bureaucrats and an endless runaround just to receive a right-to-work pass. When he finally received an identity 'pass book', which was the fulfillment of something he had desperately longed for, a white man, out of spite, tore it up in front of him saying, "Now try and find work."

> Simon said later, "So I laughed with myself. I have been trying to live a decent life and be a good citizen, but from what I have discovered, it means I am an outcast." Losing his identity book was the final straw. Simon found himself roaming the streets with the hammer.
>
> During his trial, Simon said: "I know that a white person on this earth, whether he claims to be a Christian or not, all that he prays for is that he lives for a long time and that he enjoys life. A white person does not pray to God that God causes us, irrespective of color, to live peacefully and in harmony. The whites always talk of peace when they in fact do not exercise peace."
>
> He added that when he went out to commit his crimes, he had made up his mind that he would not hurt children. ". . . So I decided, well, I should not touch the children. No matter what they were doing. I should not touch them, seeing that the children really do not know what is happening on this earth. The children will be left untouched."

ANOTHER PAINFUL CONSIDERATION

There was another painful consideration regarding the Hammerman. This was a black man. It could be so easy to have prejudice and racial hatred take root and bring deep resentment, but if we let that happen, it could destroy our efforts to reach out to the people in the township areas of our country and the surrounding nations.

Simon was sentenced to execution by hanging, a sentence

that was carried out on 20 November 1985. After much deliberation amongst both families involved and in mourning, it was decided that Jay and Terri's children would remain with Jay's sister's family that included two lovely daughters, cousins whom they love dearly.

I share this story in some detail because it was a major event, not only in our lives, but for many in South Africa, making national headlines for some time.

For Ann and me, God used this tragedy to embolden us even further. If such hatred existed, then it was even more imperative that we do all we can to bring an understanding of God's love to the people of Africa. Where there was violence and even war, we wanted to bring healing and restoration. We had dedicated ourselves to be instruments of forgiveness, love and light.

THROUGH ANN'S EYES

Given such circumstances, I sometimes had difficulty being at peace when Peter was away. It was equally hard for him to go away, leaving our children and me alone at home.

We had moved to an isolated property in a farming area outside the town of Nelspruit. There were many nights when I couldn't sleep because I heard strange noises outside and the beautiful old wooden floors in the farmhouse creaked as the nighttime temperatures fluctuated.

This situation with the Hammerman created a dilemma for both of us. Peter needed to leave town in a few days for our next outreach, something our ministry had planned far in advance. I hated that he needed to leave while I was in an uneasy state of mind, but I also didn't want to hinder the ministry.

A couple of nights after he'd left, I was once again awakened by a strange sound. Terrified, I felt like pulling the covers up over my head and hiding forever, but my love as a mother was greater than my fear. I had to make sure our children were safe.

I tiptoed to the window, pulled back the curtain, and looked out. My heart leaped into my throat as I realised someone was out there, standing off to the side of the house. Praying silently, I went to another window for another look. This time, what I saw took my breath away. A gigantic angel, much bigger than any ordinary man, stood guard at the corner of our house. I looked up toward the other corner of the house and there stood another angel, just as big.

In that instant, I knew God was watching over our children and me. Peaceful sleep soon followed.

THE LITTLE HEN

Around this time, I held meetings in Malamulele, in northern South Africa. This was an area renowned for witchcraft and demonic power. We saw many people healed and set free there, but what spoke to me was a simple way God reminded me that, no matter what evil may lurk around us, He watched over us.

Our first order of business whenever we came to a new area was to set up our various tents. We were ready to pitch the main tent when a little hen showed up, strutted right into the kitchen tent and laid an egg on the ground. We had no idea where she had come from since we were out in an open area, and there weren't any houses nearby. Someone made a funny remark about me having an egg for breakfast, and I didn't think much more about it.

The next morning, the little hen came back and laid another egg inside our kitchen tent. And the morning after that, and each day of the outreach, she did the same.

On the last day, our cook said, "Peter, have you realised how God has provided you with an egg for breakfast every day of this outreach?"

Yes, He had. Perhaps it was a little thing, but what a great example of God's love and provision, even for our smallest need.

CHAPTER 9

ARRESTED BY COMPASSION

MOZAMBIQUE, SOUTH AFRICA, 1983

Toward the end of 1983, I felt we needed to go into Mozambique. This country is along the northeastern border of South Africa with Tanzania to the north, Malawi and Zambia in the northwest and bordered by the Indian Ocean coast on the east. Vasco da Gama explored this area in 1498 and Portugal colonised it in 1505, establishing trading posts on the new European sea route to the East. After over four centuries of Portuguese rule, Mozambique gained its independence in 1975 and soon became the People's Republic of Mozambique. After only two years of independence, the country descended into an intense and protracted civil war, lasting from 1977 to 1992. This is one of the poorest and most underdeveloped countries in the world.

Going into this war-torn country was not anything I would choose to do of my own accord. At that time, Mozambique was under control of a harsh Marxist regime that had closed many churches and made it a crime to preach and encourage people to receive Jesus. Furthermore, a war of words had existed between our two countries, along with a few border skirmishes. South Africans were not allowed into Mozambique and our young soldiers fiercely patrolled this border. Our son, Wade, had become a fighter pilot in the South African Air Force, and Kevin was based in an army camp in the northeastern town of Phalabourwa in South Africa. Although they were not deployed into this area, we fully knew much of what was happening along this border.

War also raged inside the country of Mozambique, as the rebel group Renamo fought to overthrow the Frelimo government. All sides were guilty of horrible atrocities, so it was hard to tell who the good guys were—or if there were any. This was another good reason to steer clear of this country struggling to find its own way after centuries of colonialism.

The chilly relationship between our two countries suddenly thawed. Within a few months, Mozambique and South Africa came to what the local newspapers called "one of the great diplomatic breakthroughs of our time." The Nkomati Accord (Agreement of non-Aggression and Good Neighbourliness) signed in March of 1984 agreed that trade and open travel would exist between the two countries.

Within two weeks, I had a visa and was headed for Mozambique.

To my sadness and horror, I discovered that things were even worse than I had expected. In the first few hours of my trip, travelling by car on the road to the capital city of Maputo, I passed burned-out vehicles still smoldering from a rebel rocket attack. I was driving right into the jaws of danger.

In Maputo, we found a church holding onto faith amid

horrible persecution. Most of the pastors had recently been released from prison. Some were painfully thin from malnutrition. Many bore scars from beatings they had endured. One such man, Pastor Malungu, who pastored one of the biggest churches in Mozambique, suffered a beating that left him crippled.

The church members also hurt; they were hungry, ragged, sick and struggled every day just to survive, yet they were full of faith and always ready to sing. Although they didn't have enough food for their own children, they had set up a feeding program to help other needy families in their area. These people were desperately poor in the things of this world, yet I found them to be rich in the things of God.

When I returned home and told Ann what I'd seen in Mozambique, she agreed that we should soon return with a shipment of clothing, medicine and other supplies to help those in need.

LET THE STARVING BE ON YOUR HEAD

The next day, I went to the city of Nelspruit, driven by my mission to find help for the hungry. I approached various business people, asking them to donate to help the suffering children in Maputo. I visited a local bakery, told the owner what I had experienced in Mozambique and asked what his bakery did with yesterday's bread. He listened as I painted a dramatic picture of the suffering I had seen—children so frail their ribs were clearly visible through their skin, some who were half the size a child their age ought to be. Others who were so weak from hunger they could barely stand.

He remained unmoved. "Sorry. I can't help you."

"Why not?" I was taken aback. "What good is stale bread to you? Don't you throw it away?"

"No." He shook his head. "We give it to the pigs."

"Pigs?!"

He shrugged off my shock. "It's in our contract." Then he explained that his bakery had an agreement with a local piggery. Day-old bread was sold as fodder for the animals.

"But you don't understand," I insisted. "Children are *starving*."

"I'm sorry. But there's nothing I can do."

I stormed out to my car, slammed my door and turned on the ignition. Then I turned it back off. I walked back inside and stood before the bakery owner. I worked my hardest to retain my cool.

"My friend, I want to tell you something." I measured my words, keeping myself calm. "There will come a day when you will have to tell God why you gave bread to pigs when children were dying. Let that be upon your own head." Then I turned on my heels and walked out.

By the time I reached the car, I heard the owner's voice behind me. "Hey, stop a minute!" He waved me down. "I'm not prepared to take that risk. You can come and get as much bread as you need."

A couple of days later, Ann and I were on our way back to Maputo with a one-ton truck and a trailer full of stale bread and other supplies.

ROADBLOCK

We were perhaps 30 miles into Mozambique, when we stopped at a military roadblock. A half-dozen soldiers wearing camouflage uniforms and carrying assault rifles shouted commands at us.

Ann turned to me. "What do they want?"

"I have no idea."

I wasn't even sure whether they were government soldiers or rebels. I knew enough to realise that some of them were shouting in Portuguese and others in their own dialect, but I couldn't understand a word of it. We sat there in our truck knowing they wouldn't think twice about shooting us. Dozens of innocent people were murdered in Mozambique every day.

One soldier gestured, and I pulled the truck forward a few feet—and really set them off. They yelled as if they thought we were trying to run from the roadblock. One of them pointed his weapon at us. I held up my hands and tensed as I prepared to feel the bullets rip into my body. But when the soldier saw I wasn't trying to be difficult, he slowly lowered his weapon.

In response to his shouts, a big, burly captain came out of the nearby tent carrying a 15-pound sledgehammer. Glaring angrily, he strode straight toward Ann's side of the truck. Ann's face ashened. A small cry escaped her lips. I knew she was thinking about her sister's death at the hands of the Hammerman.

I leaned in. "Roll down your window. I'll try to reason with him."

She shook her head. "I can't."

I reached over to roll the window down myself, hoping to stop him before he swung his hammer and showered us with broken glass.

Anger flashed in his eyes. He took aim at the side of the truck.

"No!" I held up my hands in protest. "Don't."

Ann gasped as the man drew back his arms to strike. The soldiers egged him on.

Suddenly, amid all the confusion, I realised that the front of our truck was slightly past the poles that had been erected on the sides of the road. I slowly shifted into reverse gear and backed up a few feet.

In an instant, everything changed. The soldiers, who had been so angry and threatening only a few moments ago, smiled and nodded at us as if they were welcoming us to their country. A matter of a few feet had made all the difference in the world. They had been ready to kill us, simply because we had gone slightly past their boundary.

Within five minutes, we were on our way, breathing deep sighs of relief and thanking God for getting us through another death-defying situation—one of many we would face in this war-torn nation.

A little further down the road, we drove past a burning truck. A few kilometres past that, we needed to stop to let several enormous Russian-made tanks cross the roadway. Destruction and violence surrounded us. Yet in my heart I knew this was where we needed to be.

OPENING CLOSED DOORS

By God's grace, we made it to Maputo, and the people were delighted to receive the gifts we brought. The bread was a bit stale, but to stomachs burning with hunger, it was like manna from heaven.

Now I turned my attention to accomplishing what God had sent me to do in Mozambique: Preach the Gospel. God had told me that I would preach in every city of that country, and that He would bring a great revival. I couldn't wait.

Through contacts in the local church, I managed to set up a meeting with the National Director of Religious Affairs, Dr. Chambal. When I went to meet him, I took along videos of our outreaches, a VCR and a monitor and several of our publications. I wanted him to understand that we had not come to Mozambique to stir up trouble, but to serve as ambassadors of Christ.

Dr. Chambal listened as I explained that God had sent me to Mozambique to preach about God's love. He watched the videos. He thumbed through the materials. Then he told me that although he was happy that I had such concern for his country, it was illegal to preach the Gospel in Mozambique. He said, "It is my duty to tell you that if you even share the Gospel with one person on the street, you will be arrested."

I left his office feeling dejected and demoralised. God had given me Revelation 3:8 as a scripture to stand on: "See, I have set before you an open door, and no one can shut it." But the first man I met with had slammed it closed.

I stood outside wondering what I should do next. I felt in

my heart I should go back to the director again, so I returned and asked his secretary if I could have one more minute of his time. He graciously agreed.

"Just tell me," I said as I entered the room, "is there any other way I can help?"

The director contemplated for a moment then said, "Many people in our country are starving. If there is any way you could provide food, that would be an enormous help."

I told him I'd be happy to do that and that it would be helpful if I could get a closer look at the situation.

"Of course. Can you come back in two weeks?"

SURROUNDED BY SUFFERING

I did as he asked, and two weeks later, I found myself in a government aircraft, flying up to the coastal town of Vilanculos. From there, we drove 20 kilometres into the interior of the country, to the village of Pambarra. My understanding was that I would be there for one day to have a quick look at the situation, so I hadn't brought any clothes or personal items with me. After dropping me off, the pilot said he was flying to a nearby city to refuel, and would be back shortly. I expected him to return in a few hours.

He didn't return.

I found myself stranded in Pambarra, surrounded by unbelievable suffering.

Desperate mothers clutched their dying children to their breasts, crying and pleading for something to eat. Some of these women had carried their children for days to reach this place because they had heard they could find food there. It was a false hope. The government operated what they called a "Food Distribution Center" at Pambarra, but there was no food.

Each day, more than 30 people died around me, many of them children, and I could do nothing about it. I wept as someone handed me a shovel. I helped dig graves for mass burials—shallow trenches in the sand into which we buried dozens of bodies at once. There was neither time nor strength to dig individual graves, and the dead had to be buried quickly to prevent the spread of disease.

Death hung in the air like a great, silent, eerie cloud. Thirty thousand people crowded into a small area, and yet they made little noise. The camp was full of children too weak from hunger to run or play. There was no laughter from children playing, no murmur of conversation. The eyes that looked in mine were full of desperation. They had given up hope.

Day after day after day, the horror gnawed at me. My emotions were so crushed by everything I saw, smelled and experienced that I felt as if my heart was being shredded into tiny pieces. The fear of arrest in this country waned in the light of the compassion that had arrested my heart.

It was incredible to me that most South Africans knew nothing about the suffering taking place in Mozambique. We were a rich country, yet our neighbours were suffering and dying. We remained oblivious and did nothing to help them. It amazed me to see how we could go about our lives, looking out for ourselves, and never even notice the suffering around us.

"DO WHAT YOU CAN DO, AND I WILL BE WITH YOU."

Five days had passed and I had no way to let Ann know I was all right. As far as she knew, rebel rockets shot down our airplane. I knew that by now she had made dozens of phone calls trying to get information and listened to every newscast in case there was a report of a plane going down, but she would have heard nothing. I was distressed to think about what she and our children must be going through, and wondered when, if ever, the pilot would return.

That day an elderly man stumbled out of the brush and into the village clearing. Hunger had weakened him so much he could barely lift his feet. He kicked up dust as he shuffled forward.

I ran to him, put my arm around him and helped him into the shade of a big tree. He was as light as a feather. I helped him sit with his back against the tree.

"I'll get you some water," I promised. "I'll be right back."

I knew he needed more than a drink, but that was all I could offer: a cup of dirty water.

I ran through the village, grabbed a cup and filled it with water, then I hurried back to find the old man asleep. I tapped him on the shoulder, but he did not respond. I tapped again, harder this time, and his head rolled to the side. He was dead.

Something inside of me snapped. A rush of anger coursed through my veins. I looked to the sky, my raspy voice rising. "Why did You bring me here?! You called me to preach, but I can't preach to these people, and I can't help them without food. I can't take this anymore! Is this your will?! My heart is broken . . . "

The man's lifeless body beside me, I wept in anger and frustration. "The worst is that I don't even know how You feel. I don't know if this is Your will, or if it means anything to You that these people are dying. I really *need* to *know*."

As I continued to weep, I felt God's gentle voice inside me. *My son, My heart is broken, too. I feel what you feel, only much more deeply. It is not My will that these people should die like this; I want to help them. That is why I sent you here.*

"But God," I cried, "what do you want me to do? I don't have any food, and I don't have any money."

God certainly knew that was true. He saw how Ann and I struggled just to get by. He had heard me pray every single month, time and again, just to receive finances so our ministry could continue.

"Why don't you send someone who has money?" I argued. Clearly, He picked the wrong man.

His response was quick and firm: *Do what you can do, and I will be with you.*

I sighed. "I'll try. That's all I can do."

Beneath that tree, I felt so weak and helpless. Sitting there, I never could have imagined that one day we would feed more than a million hungry children every day.

Five days later, our pilot returned to take us back to Maputo. He explained that he had been gone so long because there was no fuel, but he had promised to come back, and here he was. I felt a rush of relief that I'd be able to get back to Ann and the children.

As we taxied down the bumpy landing strip, I realised that my life had changed forever. Even today, as I look back on what I went through during those 10 days in Pambarra, I realise that it had more impact on me than anything else I've ever experienced.

Before that, I had seen myself as a practical person, led by my head more than my heart. But seeing those people suffering and dying had changed me. I had experienced true compassion for people, and ever since then, I cannot pray for anyone simply out of a sense of duty.

From the air, I looked down on Pambarra and saw that it looked so peaceful and picturesque, a sub-tropical paradise of little thatched huts. It was only when you got close that you could see the suffering that lay beneath. I knew the same was true of human beings. If you want to help them, you need to get close enough to see and understand what they are going through.

When I arrived home, I grabbed Ann, and we held each other so tightly that it was hard to let go. Ann had been so worried that I was lying dead or injured in some remote part of Mozambique . . . and what I had seen in Mozambique had shaken me to the core. I was no stranger to suffering or violence, yet I had never encountered anything that had moved me so deeply.

Ann searched my eyes. "Peter, what's wrong with you? Something's changed."

I shook my head. "There's nothing wrong with me. But

everything has changed."

A new sense of urgency burned within me. I couldn't get those suffering people out of my mind. Every time I closed my eyes, I saw their faces. I had to get back with help as soon as possible.

I said to Ann, "Darling, either I need to forget what I just experienced, or you and I need to commit our lives to helping those children. This is an opportunity to demonstrate the Gospel that we preach. I want to make a difference."

And with that, God added another dimension to our calling. We emptied the little bit we had in our personal savings accounts to buy food, medicine, blankets and other essentials. We took out a loan to buy more, and we called everyone we knew. Within a few days we were on our way back to Pambarra with three truckloads of 80 tons of lifesaving assistance.

It was a dangerous trip. Most of the way, we travelled under the protection of a government military convoy. Several times we came under fire from rebel snipers. The Bible says, "Let us not grow weary while doing good," (Galatians 6:9) and on this long, scary trip through a war zone, I understood why. Sometimes, doing good is the hardest thing in the world. It would have been easy to turn and run the other way, but God's love would not let us do that.

A celebration erupted when we drove those trucks into Pambarra, after three long days on the road. Seeing the light of hope come into starving people's lives gave me a wonderful feeling that is indescribable. As we unloaded the trucks, I realised that 80 tons of food and supplies had looked like so much when we left South Africa . . . but as the trucks emptied, I saw it wasn't much at all. We needed to do more, much more. It was a small start, but at least it was a start.

Ann and I knew we needed to focus our attention on the lives that were being saved, and not on the ones we couldn't reach. We couldn't allow the enormity of the problem to overwhelm us. We couldn't save everybody—but we could save some.

PREACHING THROUGH OUR ACTIONS

Many years have passed since I first arrived in Pambarra, but time has not dimmed the memory of the horror I encountered there. 1984 was the year of the terrible famine in Ethiopia that killed an estimated 1 million people. During that same year, hundreds of thousands also died in countries like Mozambique, although most of the suffering took place far away from TV cameras and the news media.

One of the most heartbreaking things about Pambarra was that there were more than 300 orphans there with nobody to care for them. Many of them had been brought to Pambarra by parents who had since died. Children as young as three or four years old were alone in the world. They had no one to respond to their hunger cries. In many cases, the parents had died because they had given what little food they had to their children.

I knew in my heart that we needed to build a home to care for those innocent victims of war and drought. That was the beginning of our Pambarra Life Centre and orphanage. It was also the start of a new chapter in our work which would later be known as *JAM—Joint Aid Management, International—* dedicated to "Helping Africa Help Itself."

We were showing the people of Mozambique that we cared about them, and that opened the door for us to preach the Gospel in that country. We were learning that the Gospel is not ministered in word only, but in the demonstration of the love we preach. It's true that people don't care what you know until they know that you care. A famous quote resonated in me, "Preach the gospel at all times, and when necessary use words."

By the end of the year, I had persuaded Dr. Chambal to give us permission to conduct an outreach in the city of Maputo. Because of our humanitarian work in Pambarra, he readily agreed. The only stipulation was that the outreach could not be held on government land or in a public building. He insisted, in fact, that if I was going to preach, it "had to be in a church."

Surprisingly, in a country that had done everything within its power to oppose Christianity, it didn't take long to find the perfect venue for our outreach. An old aircraft hangar near the city airport had been converted into a church that could hold over 8,000 people.

When I told Dr. Chambal where we wanted to hold the outreach, he rolled his eyes. "Why do you want such a big place?" he asked. "Only four or five hundred people ever come to any type of religious meeting."

"Not this one," I assured him. "Many people are going to come."

He shot me a look that was a mixture of amusement and

pity. He probably didn't know whether to laugh at me or feel sorry for me because I was so delusional.

"Okay," he finally said. "I will sign the papers. You can hold your outreach there."

He didn't say it, but I was fairly certain I knew that he was thinking: "Don't be surprised if nobody shows up."

CHAPTER 10

GOVERNMENTS TAKE NOTICE

MOZAMBIQUE & SWAZILAND, SOUTH AFRICA, 1983

It is an undisputable fact that the church grows stronger during times of persecution. History shows that there is strength and power in the blood of martyrs. That proved true in the Soviet Union and Eastern Europe during the 20th century, and in the 21st century, the church thrives under severe persecution in China. I was about to discover that the same was true in Mozambique.

On the first night of our Maputo outreach, we arrived an hour before the service was due to start. People had packed the hanger to capacity. The atmosphere buzzed with excitement and anticipation.

For many years, Christians in Mozambique couldn't gather in large groups. The government had forced an atheist doctrine on the people, believing that faith in God was nothing but antiquated superstition. The government regularly jailed pastors and "advised" them that belief in God was not permitted. The church was demoralised and beaten down. On top of this, people starved. It seemed every family I met in Mozambique had lost at least one loved one to hunger. Amazingly, the suffering they endured had not extinguished their faith in God.

That night in the hanger, the people gathered, expecting God to meet them, and He did. Blind eyes saw. Crippled legs grew strong. Tumours vanished. Children laughed with glee as deaf ears opened and they heard their parents' voices. Mothers wept with joy when they saw their children's faces for the first time.

News of these miracles quickly spread throughout the city and into the surrounding communities. By the third night of the outreach, the large crowds couldn't fit inside the building. Thousands crowded outside, banging on the windows and metal doors, trying to get in. Some of them even climbed up the walls and sat on the rafters. It was a dangerous situation, because the trusses were not designed to carry the weight of 30–40 people sitting on each one.

Thankfully, the building survived these stresses and so did our evangelistic team, although we were all completely drained and exhausted by the time we fell into bed that night.

The following night was more of a challenge. Thousands of people had come seeking prayer for healing, with friends and family having carried them there. There were probably a thousand men, women and children lying on the floor at the front of the hall, suffering from every imaginable disease and deformity. A horrible stench filled the hall, most of it from those poor, sick people.

After preaching, I arranged four healing lines and literally ran up and down each line, laying hands on the people as I prayed for the sick.

That's when God did the most amazing thing I had ever seen up to that point. As I rushed from one sick person to the next, laying hands on them and praying for them, the entire crowd suddenly erupted in excitement. I looked up to see a woman I had prayed for earlier that week. She had been bedridden for 18 years, completely paralyzed. And although her friends had carried her to every service so far, she had not been healed.

Now she was *standing* on her wooden stretcher, swaying on her feet as if she were about to collapse. Then, she screamed with joy, shouting out that God had healed her. The next thing I knew, she jumped off her stretcher and ran across the front of the hall, shouting and praising God.

What happened next changed my understanding and my perspective of God. All around me, sick and crippled people struggled to rise as faith stirred in them. They saw what God had done for this woman, and they believed He *could* and *would* do the same for them. Some dragged themselves across the floor, trying with every ounce of strength they had to rise and walk.

One man threw his crutches away, tried to take a step and fell on his face. A counsellor rushed to him, helped him to his feet and attempted to give his crutches back.

"No!" He shoved the crutches away. "I'm going to walk."

Once again, he tried to take a step, and once again he fell to the concrete floor.

"Help me up!" he cried. The counsellor did as he asked, and then stepped away to give him another try.

He kicked his leg out, and it looked like he was going down again. But then he took one step . . . and then another . . . as the power of God surged through his body. Within a few minutes, he had teamed up with the woman who had been paralysed, and ran around as if they'd had nothing wrong with them.

Another little lady whose feet were pointed the wrong way had huge calluses on them from crawling along on the ground and dragging her useless legs behind her. Now she jumped up and down, her feet still callused, but otherwise perfectly healed.

That night, 12 people who had been crippled were healed, *with no one laying hands on them or praying over them.* They were all healed in a sovereign act of God.

THE LAST STRAW

I should have known that what was happening in Maputo would not sit well with the atheistic government of Mozambique. It was fine with them if we wanted to hold a small, religious gathering in a corner of the city where nobody would notice. But this meeting had caused an uproar throughout the entire city—and that would not be tolerated.

In the Bible, the Scribes and Pharisees often reacted in anger when Jesus performed a miracle. Instead of being thrilled that the power of God had helped the poor and the sick, they became enraged that their authority had been challenged. This was just more of the same.

The very next day, we received a call from the government, requesting the names and addresses of the 12 people who had been healed so dramatically the night before. Although we did not have the names and addresses of them all, we did manage to provide personal information for seven people, and they were summoned to meet with the local authorities.

A group of local pastors accompanied them. I was not permitted to attend.

One pastor told me later that the little woman whose feet had been turned around could not control her joy and excitement. She kept jumping up and down, shouting, "Look what God has done for me!"

Still not able to accept the truth, the officials then went with those people to the hospitals where they had been treated and requested to see their medical records, to confirm that they had all really been crippled. The national newspaper reported all of this the following day, but the article was written in a mocking tone: "There is a man from South Africa claiming to be the Saviour and healing the sick," the reporter wrote. And yet, to his credit, he acknowledged each miracle.

The writer clearly did not mean to promote the outreach or stir up faith in the public, but that is what he did. The night after the news story appeared, a massive crowd turned out. I have no idea how many people came, but I am convinced it would have overflowed a soccer stadium, and we only had room for 8,000. The vast crowd blocked the main road leading from the airport into the city of Maputo. Hundreds of people stood in the road, and there was no way for cars to get around them.

That was the last straw as far as the government was concerned. Early the next morning, our friend from the Bureau of Religious Affairs showed up with a simple message: "Stop the meetings now."

I protested that we would try to find a way to keep the crowds under control, but he stood his ground. "No. There will be no meeting tonight."

By now, I knew from personal experience that no man could stop God from doing what He planned. If He wanted me to preach the Gospel in Mozambique, and I knew He did, there was no way a government edict would keep me from doing so. If this door closed, God would open another. It was that simple.

It just so happened that a man second in charge to the Governor of the Sofala Province flew his blind son from the city of Beira to Maputo. He too was healed. The father said, "You need to bring this thing that God is doing to my city!" He was so grateful that he promised to do everything within his power to get permission for us to hold an outreach in Beira. Although he was not a Christian, he could not deny what God had done for his child.

Within a few weeks of our meetings in Maputo being shut down, we were invited to preach in Beira. And there was more good news. We would be allowed to use the rustic basketball arena in the middle of the city which seated around 20,000 people.

Like elsewhere in Mozambique, we encountered soldiers carrying assault rifles, some with grenades strung around their necks. Danger lurked around every corner. The weak electric power went out several times each day and sometimes stayed off for many hours. We never knew from one moment to the next what might happen. And yet, amid such violence, uncertainty and danger, there we were, holding another public outreach and preaching about the healing power of Jesus.

The people of Beira were just as hungry for God as the citizens of Maputo had been. The first night, the arena was filled to capacity, and the air seemed to be charged with electric anticipation.

How beautiful it was to hear those 20,000 people lift their voices in song to God. Many of them had suffered terribly. Some had lost legs or arms to landmines; others had lost husbands, wives or children to the violence and war. I doubt if there was anyone in the arena who hadn't suffered in some way. Yet they sang with such fervency and joy. It was incredible!

Just as I was getting up to preach, I heard someone shouting angrily. I looked in the direction of the commotion and was startled to see an entire platoon of heavily armed government soldiers striding into the arena. The officer in charge seemed to be half drunk as he swaggered up to me.

"This meeting is closed," he shouted. "These people must disperse."

He held up a telex that he had received from Maputo, revoking my permission to hold an outreach in Beira, stating that we could not gather in this public place.

I gestured at the microphone. "Will you tell the people?"

He folded his arms across his chest. "No. It would cause a riot. You must tell them."

I had no choice but to obey.

I stepped to the microphone and announced, "I am sorry to

advise you that this meeting has been closed by order of the government. Please leave quietly. We will try our best to get permission again." Amazingly, the people left almost without a murmur of protest. They had seen enough to know that any resistance would likely be met with a show of force.

By God's grace, we had a strong ally who had arranged for us to come to Beira. He took the matter to the Head Justice of Mozambique's Supreme Court who, although a Muslim, agreed to intervene with the central government.

THROUGH ANN'S EYES

I was excited to join Peter and our team in Beira, but soon after we arrived, I regretted it. The scrutiny of the armed officials at every meeting unnerved me. Because Mozambique is a neighbouring country to the east of South Africa, one might think that we were in a familiar environment and culture, but not at all! The modern cities of South Africa, where electricity is available at the touch of a switch and clean water comes at the turn of a tap, are a long, long way from Beira.

We were housed in a tiny apartment that didn't even have glass in the windows. In place of the glass were old pieces of hard, stiff, plastic sheeting that had become brittle from the heat of the harsh African sun.

The lack of cleanliness was obvious and made me uncomfortable, yet I came to realise that when necessities are in short supply, food comes before soap. I tried my best to smile and act as if everything was fine, but everything felt so alien and frightening—especially at night. Nearly every evening we heard the booming echoes of heavy artillery explosions mixed with the staccato sounds of assault rifle fire. It was the most disturbing experience to lie in bed and listen to the sounds of battle happening all around us. Before that, I had only experienced such an event at the movies.

We knew the war raged within five to seven miles from where we slept, but one night I woke up to a terrible racket that seemed to be right at our window. Almost petrified with fear, I got out of bed and took my flashlight to investigate. To my amazement, many giant-sized flying roaches had become trapped between the crisp, sun-baked plastic sheets on the window frame. They ran up and down looking for a way to get out, making so much noise that it sounded like an army of rats!

They were just bugs, but with my nerves on edge from the gunfire, all I wanted to do was pack up and head for home, away from that dirty, mosquito-infested place. But I didn't. I remember thinking that I was not raised for this or prepared for this. Thankfully, I managed to focus on the reason we were there rather than the tough circumstances that surrounded us.

ALL HEAVEN BREAKS LOOSE

While we waited hoping to receive our permit, I preached in a church on Sunday. A crippled woman arrived on crutches, came forward for prayer and Jesus healed her. Two days later we heard that she was the niece of the Governor. She went to him to show him how Jesus had healed her—and now the Governor was on our side too.

Then came good news from Maputo. A telex arrived stating

that our outreach had been reapproved, with two stipulations. First, the meetings must be held in a church, rather than a public venue. Second, we could not lay hands on the sick "because the laying on of hands is proving so popular with the people that it is distracting from the ruling party's popularity in the country."

Of course, this was not the first time someone had told me to stop laying hands on the sick. To me, this opposition was simply a testimony to the power of this practise. God had demonstrated again and again that His power was not limited by whether or not we could lay hands on the sick.

The real problem we faced was that the biggest church in the city could hold only about 400 people, and we knew at least 20,000 would likely show up because they'd already done so.

Thankfully, I had an idea. I enquired from the authorities if the property that *belonged* to a church was considered part of the church. In other words, could people gather *outside* the church building, so long as they were standing on church property?

The answer came back, "Yes, people can gather on the grounds surrounding the church."

That's all we needed to hear. Sure, only a tiny percentage of those who came to the meetings would be able to see me, but what did that matter? Romans 10:17 says that, "faith *comes* by hearing, and hearing by the word of God." We set up several outdoor speakers so people could hear the message broadcast from the outer walls of the church building. What happened next was, as always, up to God.

It wasn't legal to advertise the meeting, but people still

arrived by the thousands. Several hours before the service, the church pews were filled. Then the yard around the church filled. Then hundreds perched atop the walls surrounding the church property. Then the trees surrounding the property filled with people. They even crammed onto the balconies of surrounding buildings. The government's decision to shut down our first outreach hadn't discouraged anyone from coming to this one. If anything, this crowd was larger than the one that had packed the basketball arena.

Only one thing dampened my enthusiasm: several government officials sat on the front row, scrutinizing every move I made. I knew they were prepared to shut us down in a moment if I did anything they perceived to be beyond the letter of the law. They were particularly concerned that I may lay hands on the sick. Those skeptical, hard-edged government observers were in for a night they would never forget!

It began when I prayed for those who wanted to surrender to Christ. During the prayer, the power of God fell on an entire section of the crowd in the yard, sending about 500 people sprawling to the ground.

Those bureaucrats were on the scene immediately, notebooks in hand, demanding to know what was going on. Some of them were clearly frightened by what they saw. They had never encountered anything like this before.

While they were still trying to get things "under control," a scream erupted from the back of the yard where a bunch of hands lifted an empty wheelchair high into the air. The woman who had once sat in that wheelchair now pushed her way through the crowd toward the platform on legs that had not worked in many years. It wasn't easy for her to get to the front because the people were so densely packed. Her triumphant march took about 10 minutes—but she was determined to show everyone what God had done for her, including those the government had sent.

After that, all *heaven* broke loose!

Dozens of people were healed spontaneously, many of whom came forward to testify about what God had done for them. Thousands of people received salvation. God was doing even more than we had seen when we were free to lay hands on the people. It was an awesome display of God's love and power.

Throughout the week, things got wilder. So many came that even the vacant piece of land alongside the church was packed with people. They couldn't see what was going on, but they could hear the message. They had come in faith, expecting that God would meet them—and He did.

This could have caused problems with the government, because those people were not standing on property that belonged to the church. The authorities could have used it as an excuse to shut us down, but they didn't. The meetings went on for a full week, as planned. Representatives of the government were present every night, observing and taking notes, but not one ever made a move to intervene. I felt certain that they must have been touched by what they saw and heard. But if they were, they never dared to show it.

ANSWERING TO CHARGES

The day after our outreach meetings closed, I received a telex from an angry Director of Religious Affairs. I was to appear in Maputo immediately to answer charges that I was in Mozambique illegally.

"This is very serious." The bureaucrat leaned back in his chair and glared at me over the top of his glasses. "You have not been honest with us about your reasons for coming into Mozambique."

"I don't know what you mean," I protested. "Why would I do something like that?"

He moved forward and read from an official-looking document on his desk. "In your visa application, you said you wanted to come into Mozambique to help the poor." He suggested that we had obtained our visas by fraud, since we had really come into the country intending to hold an evangelistic crusade. "That means you are in our country illegally."

"But we had permission—"

"You have the wrong type of visa," he interrupted.

I tried to explain that I didn't even know there were different types of visas, but he wasn't willing to listen.

He slid an envelope across the desk in my direction. I opened it and withdrew a letter, written on government stationery by the Minister of Justice, stating that I was not permitted to preach any more in Mozambique, nor was I to ask for permission to hold any more outreaches. The government saw the value of what we were doing among the orphans and other suffering children there, otherwise we would have been kicked out of the country completely.

Either way, once again the door had been slammed in my face, and it felt like a terrible blow. I tried to find some comfort by recalling that God had told me I would preach in every city in Mozambique, and that there would be a great revival.

Still, I was heartbroken. God had given me a great compassion for the suffering people of the country, and it grieved me deeply not to be able to tell them about God's great love.

THE GOD WHO PROVIDES

Despite our setback with the government, God seemed to be doing miracles on every side. We had heard of some 550 people in a village deep in Gaza Province who desperately needed food. We took a seven-ton 4x4 truck loaded to the top with corn and headed toward the village. It was a two-hour drive through dangerous territory, even though we had several government soldiers armed with AK rifles and bazookas sitting on top of the food. The road was in terrible condition, but we finally arrived at the village. To our astonishment there were more than 2,000 people there, not the 550 people we expected.

People from the surrounding villages had heard food was coming, and they walked for miles to get there. "Bush telegraph" is amazing. The soldiers said we should leave without distributing the food because we did not have enough and opening the food would cause a riot amongst these desperate people. They were right about the food being too little. We needed at least four times what we had, but I could not leave.

We prayed. I asked the soldiers to get the people to sit in

rows and not move until we had completed serving the rations. We placed the food in front of them and did not change the measure of the ration we used. We couldn't. We only had one measure with us. We started distributing and—to our amazement—we didn't stop until we had given everyone a full ration. When we finished, there were still 12 bags of maize left over. Those we used to bless the soldiers.

When we arrived back in Maputo, I calculated the food it should have taken to feed the people and it was over 22 tons. We had only around 7 tons. The Bible records incidents where Jesus fed the 5,000 people with just two loaves and a few fishes, and also how God used Elijah to multiply the widow's last portion of oil and flour, yet we couldn't help but be in awe of experiencing a new miracle from our God of miracles.

A TRIP OVERSEAS

Even though we saw miracles every day, financial pressures continued to rise. Between that and the heartbreak of being told that we could no longer hold outreaches in Mozambique, Ann and I both felt like the sky was falling. Right in the middle of this, Rodney Lloyd, a pastor and Bible School lecturer from America, came to minister for our pastor, Ray McCauley, in South Africa. He and his wife Nita wanted to visit the mission field, so they accompanied us on a trip to Maputo. They were touched by what we were doing and what God was doing in us so they invited us to come to North America. Rodney kindly set up some speaking engagements for us so we could share our vision and raise support for our work in Mozambique. I was embarrassed to tell him that there was no way we could travel to America because we didn't have money for airfare.

Or did we?

We had started a savings account a few years earlier because we had always wanted to go to Israel. It wasn't much, but when we checked our balance, we found we had just enough to purchase one economy-class ticket. Only three days before we were to leave, a payment came from Ann's father's estate and we were able to buy a second ticket. It was another miracle, and I was certain God was leading us.

And so, in April 1985, we arranged for my parents to take care of our younger children. Ann and I headed out of Johannesburg on a flight across the Atlantic to Toronto, the first stop on our three-week trip. Between the two of us, we had less than $100 in cash. We truly stepped out in faith!

Our first night in Toronto, our hosts booked us in a rather nice hotel. The notice posted on the back of our room door, displaying checkout time and other pertinent information, also recorded the daily room rate of $120.

I turned to Ann. "Darling, if we have to pay the bill for this room, we're sunk." We didn't even have enough money for one night. "I just hope the church is going to pay."

We both felt great relief when the church we were visiting not only paid our hotel bill, but also blessed us with two generous financial gifts: One for the work of our ministry in Africa, and one for our personal use. Then they took us shopping in a beautiful underground mall. Although they kept urging us to buy something for ourselves, we couldn't do it. We hadn't come to North America to shop. We'd come to raise funds for children and their families who were starving, physically and spiritually.

Given the poverty we faced every day, it was troubling to see the luxurious lifestyle that the Christians in the U.S. and Canada enjoyed. We couldn't comprehend how Christians could be comfortable eating in fancy restaurants or driving top-of-the-line cars when there were so many people in the world who were suffering and who didn't know about the love of Christ.

From Canada, we travelled to Detroit, where we stayed in the home of Rodney and Nita Lloyd, who became some of our dearest friends. We enjoyed the comfort of their son, Michael's, bedroom. Other than in a toyshop, I had never seen so many toys in one place!

Their congregation welcomed us with open arms. But when I saw everything those families had—all the clothes in their closets, the expensive furnishings, the fancy cars and their beautiful homes—it ignited a moral dilemma in my heart that I struggled with for quite some time.

THROUGH ANN'S EYES

Although I loved to see all that Canada and America offered, Peter and I were so desperate to help the poor that it became a difficult situation for us. I wondered, "God, how can Your people on one side of the world be so blessed, and on the other side, be suffering so terribly?" I felt like a beggar in disguise. As we wrestled with feelings of anger and frustration, God helped us to understand.

He led me to 2 Corinthians 8:13–14: "For *I do* not mean that others should be eased and you burdened; but by an equality, *that* now at this time your abundance *may supply* their lack, that their abundance also may *supply* your lack—that there may be equality."

Paul describes a circle of blessing that results from giving and receiving. The poor are blessed through gifts provided by the wealthy. Food, clothing, and shelter become tangible expressions of God's love. And the poor, in turn, bless those who give to them, through the opportunity they have to fulfil God's purpose in their lives—as Jesus instructed, "for I was hungry and you gave Me food . . . drink . . . took Me in . . . clothed Me . . . visited Me . . . came to Me" (Matthew 25:35–36).

Our entire perspective changed as we realised that God had blessed these countries so they could help alleviate the terrible suffering that was taking place in countries like Mozambique. We also understood that African believers could return the blessing, not only through their prayers, but also through their example of faith, of trust in God and of perseverance through suffering.

We took hands and prayed, asking God to make us a "hosepipe" through which He would channel His blessings to bring an equality. We felt God speak to our hearts that this is what we would be—a conduit that allowed people in America to help our beloved Africa.

We felt an instant relief in our hearts and found many Canadian and American Christians to be cheerful givers. We returned to Africa with enough money to keep our work going for the next few months. I tried not to think too far ahead, knowing that our future was in God's hands.

OTHER CHALLENGES PEOPLE FACE

Besides our own challenges in Africa, we found that some ministers in America faced challenges of their own. One of those was a pastor we'd gotten to know a while back who had made a mistake and quickly been denounced by his church. Though he'd brought it on himself, I wasn't prepared to let him go through the battle alone. I gave him a job and ultimately brought him and his wife to South Africa so they could be restored. They needed to get away from critics and get somewhere with accountability. I assured them that by living in a safe place where they could be accepted instead of criticised, God could still use them. Showing them hope rather than the uncompassionate judgment they'd been receiving brought them to a point of true restoration.

This eventually led to an open door for us . . . one that would come years later.

MIRACLE IN SWAZILAND

We returned home and despite many hours of prayer that God would change the hearts of Mozambique's leaders and allow us to resume preaching there, that door remained closed. We were allowed to continue working with the poor, and we did our best to show Jesus' love through our acts of service. Every step of the way, the government watched us closely. One wrong move, and our work there would have been shut down.

Largely because we could not preach the Gospel in Mozambique, we decided to hold meetings in the neighbouring country of Swaziland. I didn't realise it, but God was using the difficult situation in Mozambique to widen our perspective to include all of Africa. It truly was a case of seeing "all things work together for good" (Romans 8:28).

We set up our large tent at an area called Big Bend, and it was there that I witnessed one of the greatest miracles I had ever seen. Every night, when I invited those who needed prayer to come forward, a young mother came, leading a little boy by the hand. He seemed to be about eight years old, and I could tell by the way he walked that he could not see. I found out later that the boy had been born blind. Not only had he never seen his mother's face, but he could not even distinguish light from darkness.

For 13 nights, this mother brought her young son for prayer. And every night, she went away disappointed. I knew she was devastated. I too wanted so badly to see this child healed, but it hadn't happened. What made it worse was the knowledge that this child's condition meant he had almost no hope for a decent future. In poor African countries, it can be difficult for an *able*-bodied person to build a decent life. For someone who is blind or crippled, it is almost impossible. Unless God restored his vision, this child would likely become a beggar someday, depending on the generosity of others, and perhaps dying at an early age. It broke my heart to think about it.

On the fourteenth and final night of our outreach, as I did every night, I invited those who wanted prayer to come forward. I noticed that mother moving slowly down the aisle, clutching her son to her chest, tears running down her cheeks. I knew why she was crying. This was the last meeting and she had come faithfully every night, trusting God for a miracle and nothing had happened. This was her last chance to see her son healed.

I felt great compassion for her and sensed how Jesus' heart ached for her. I walked over to her, reached out and gently opened the boy's eyelids to get a better look at the problem. My heart caught in my throat. Where his eyes should have been, there was nothing but white, bubbly blisters. There was no sign of a pupil or cornea.

I tried not to reveal my shock, but my mind was reeling. "God, how can I pray for this child to see when he doesn't even have any eyes? We need a creative miracle."

At that moment, the words of Jesus echoed through my mind: "If you ask anything in My name, I will do it" (John 14:14).

I placed my fingers on the child's eyelids and prayed a simple prayer. "Jesus, in your name, please give this child new eyes."

As I took my hands away, his eyes blinked open.

I knew immediately that he was healed as he looked at me with two beautiful, big brown eyes. A smile of delight spread across his little face. He gazed up at his mother, with an expression of absolute joy and whispered, "Mommy, you are so beautiful."

The woman hugged her son tight to her chest and sobbed deep, heartfelt tears of joy. And I wept right along with her. What a wonderful moment!

Experiencing miracles of God changes a person forever.

Before I met Jesus, I searched for something real, something to believe in and give myself to, and I had always been disappointed. Yet to see a blind child healed in an instant by the power of God, how could anything in the world ever be better than that?

Later that night, I lay awake on my bed for hours, too excited to sleep. The air around me seemed to be filled with the love and power of God. I was exhilarated by the joy of His presence. I whispered into the darkness, "You are so wonderful, Jesus. In just the twinkling of an eye, you changed that little boy's life forever!"

The next day, our last in Swaziland, our entire evangelistic team paused for a few moments to watch some kids playing soccer. There, in the midst of them, was this young child who had been healed the night before. He didn't know much about soccer, having never seen this game before, yet he was having the time of his life, running around the field like a whirlwind, just being a normal child for the first time.

It was a thrilling sight.

Amidst this joyful experience, I carried a sadness to think that there were so many in Mozambique who were in need of God's touch just like this boy, but who were being denied it because we could not get permission from the government.

That was about to change . . . but not before dodging a few more bullets.

CHAPTER 11

BULLETS WHISTLING IN THE TREES

MOZAMBIQUE, SOUTH AFRICA, 1985–1986

We couldn't hold gospel outreaches and preach in Mozambique, but thankfully, the government said our visas still allowed us to enter to assist the poor. For the next couple of years, we often drove back and forth from our home in Nelspruit to Maputo and other points in Mozambique. Every time we reached the border, I'd have to fight the fear that engulfed me because of the impending dangers I could face during the next few hours. I knew that as soon as I crossed that imaginary line, my life was at risk.

We continued to encounter burned-out shells of cars and trucks. Some were still burning or smouldering. We also continued to encounter other obstacles, including numerous military roadblocks. The worst thing about those roadblocks was that you never knew who was in charge. Were they government soldiers or rebels? It didn't matter that much because either side could be dangerous.

We often came upon roadblocks manned by a couple of non-uniformed teenagers with assault rifles and three or four hand grenades hanging on a string around their necks. It was a time of intense pressure and real, heart-thumping, stomach-clinching fear. We had no option but to completely trust in God to get us safely through.

On one occasion, as we drove into Mozambique from Swaziland, we rounded a bend in the road and came upon a Volkswagen Beetle engulfed in flames.

"Oh no!" I slammed on the brakes. "There are people in that car!" Through the flames, I could see someone frantically trying to open the driver's side door, but it would not budge. I jumped out of our truck and ran to see what I could do to help. I couldn't get closer than 15 or 20 feet because the flames were too intense. It made me sick to know that at least two people had just burned to death right in front of me. And it also frightened me to know that the rebels who had attacked the car were undoubtedly still nearby.

There was nothing I could do but get back in the truck and continue on our way, shaking with shock and grief over what I had just seen.

We knew that God was with us. If a rocket or mortar hit us, we would instantly be with Him in heaven. But that did not keep us from fearing the danger that waited around every turn.

Not long after our encounter with the burning Volkswagen, I had another close call on this same stretch of road. This time, I was alone and on my way home. It was a bright, sunny afternoon, and I bounced along on the bombed out, pockmarked road. As I drove, I constantly scanned the horizon for signs of trouble.

Up ahead, the road sloped down into a green valley. Hills

covered with scrub brush rose sharply on either side of the roadway. Relaxing for even a moment on the roads in Mozambique wasn't a luxury we had.

Suddenly I thought I saw something move. It was a couple of hundred metres in front of me, high up on the right side. I held my breath and squinted to get a better look. There it was again. As I drew closer, I could see that a rebel soldier was looking down on the roadway. The sun glinted off the barrel of his assault rifle.

He had probably seen me before I had seen him, and now he ran down the hill as fast as his legs would carry him, heading toward the spot where the road came closest to the hill.

I didn't know what to do. I couldn't outrun a bullet. And I didn't think I could get to that spot in the road before he did. Once again, I called out the same name I had shouted on that racetrack so many years ago. "Jesus!" But this time it was a heartfelt prayer. "Please help me!" I pressed down on the accelerator, but I couldn't go too fast because the torn-up road would have ripped my truck to pieces.

Ahead of me, I saw the soldier exit the brush and stand on the roadside. He lifted his rifle and prepared to shoot. I tensed, awaiting the bullet that would end my life here on earth. It never came.

To this day, I don't know what happened. Perhaps his gun jammed, perhaps he changed his mind. Perhaps he was out of ammunition. All I know for sure is that I wasn't about to go back and ask him. Jesus heard my prayer and protected me once again as I took that curve.

OUR SHIELD

A few months later, one of our trucks bringing food and other aid supplies into Mozambique came under heavy fire from a platoon of guerrilla soldiers. When that truck finally reached our base in Maputo, we counted 17 bullet holes, including three huge craters in the windscreen. Four people were riding shoulder to shoulder in the cab of that truck, and not one of them was hit or even cut by flying glass. Our people were shaking from the experience but were otherwise unscathed.

When we tried to reconstruct what had happened, we realised that one bullet had gone between the heads of two of our people. And here's what really amazed us: A bullet had hit the windscreen right in front of the driver's face. If it had come through the glass, it would have killed him. But for some reason, the bullet seemed to have bounced off the thin, plastic laminate skin that meshed the two pieces of glass together. In other words, there was a hole on the outside of the windscreen, but it did not go all the way through. Bullets fired by AK47 assault rifles will penetrate just about anything, and they leave gaping holes. But this one had bounced off. Of course, we knew the reason. The only explanation was that God had put a shield around our people.

During that same difficult season, our relief workers living at our Pambara Life Center and orphanage often found themselves caught amid violence and danger.

Once, during the middle of the night, we were aroused out of bed by the loud rat-a-tat of automatic weapons firing within a few hundred yards of our village. We quickly rounded up all the orphans and our team members, ran out into the bush and lay on the ground for what seemed like hours. We could hear the bullets whistling through the trees overhead. It was terrifying. We could even hear the breach of the rifles sliding backwards and forwards as their bullets were fired.

I was afraid that the rebels would burn our compound, which would not have been out of character for these attacks. When things quieted, all of our homes and our orphanage still stood.

The people who lived in the neighbouring village were not so fortunate. Dozens lay dead, many more wounded. The devastation was sickening. Yet again, not one of our people was harmed.

Despite the constant dangers we faced in Mozambique, we could not turn away. Too many people suffered and died.

With the help from the Lutheran Church in Germany, we appealed to the European Union for assistance. The very first year after asking for help, we received over 1,000 tons of food for starving children and their families. Within five years, we were distributing 8,000 metric tons of lifesaving food every year as well as donated, second-hand clothing.

We used the food to open several soup kitchens in the poorest areas throughout Mozambique, an endeavor that stretched our already thin budget to the breaking point.

Sadly, we discovered that some children were so dreadfully malnourished that they could not eat solid food. In fact, even the intake of our specially prepared nutritious soup mix would have been a shock to their weakened bodies. The food would have killed them. With the help of UNICEF, we found a formula to restore health to those innocent victims of famine and war. We used a simple mixture of milk, oil and sugar that we spoon-fed to the weakest children, many times a day.

We also saved lives by attaching our nutrition clinics to local hospitals. There, children weakened by hunger and especially vulnerable to dangerous, deadly diseases and malaria, could be treated.

We were learning as we progressed, and we needed to learn fast. Mothers desperately trying to feed their children from breasts that had no milk surrounded us. Some of them were so weak from hunger that they looked like walking skeletons. It shattered my heart to see the expressions on these mothers' faces as they tried and failed to feed the children they loved.

On one occasion, I sat beside one of those mothers, gently took her baby into my arms and began to pray for him. As I held him, he gasped out his last breath, and then was still.

"No! Lord, please!" But it was too late. His life had slipped away before he had even had the opportunity to enjoy it.

His mother bowed over in deep pain and wept bitterly. All I could think of was, "What if this was my child?" I could not imagine the pain this mother was experiencing.

This was such a deep life-changing experience for me and the truth suddenly came to me as a revelation: *We cannot choose where we are born. I could have been born into this family or my children could have been.*

The tragedy of it hit me.

Many times, in the course of our work, an incredible burden

of sorrow has overtaken me. It can hurt so deeply to be exposed to suffering. Whenever I'm tempted to shelter myself from the painful realities of hunger, poverty and death, I remember what an incredible privilege it is to save a life. What a joy it is to help a child come back from the brink of death.

And our own six children? They were living a life of sacrifice for the sake of us reaching these children who were in such desperate need.

Ann kept the home base going while I left for long periods of time, all the while encouraging our children that they allowed us to help so many. School meetings and sports events came and went without Dad's attendance.

This was not easy for them, but they would enjoy seeing photographs and hearing many stories from the field when I returned. It was a constant battle between wanting to protect them from the harsh realities of the pain and suffering of the people we were helping and wanting to nurture the ever-growing compassion in their hearts. During their school holidays, once the war and violence had subsided, we were able to have them accompany us on trips. They would practise their Portuguese words while interacting with the local children. Their desire to be involved in all that we were doing grew. One of the marked indications of this was when our youngest, Jackie, wanted to give her favourite, colourful "dancing dress" to a little girl who didn't own a dress.

BORN TO FLY

As we considered all the narrow escapes we'd had on Mozambique's dangerous roads, we realised that we needed an airplane. A plane would enable us to fly into remote areas that were not accessible by road. Flying would also shorten our trips, which meant we'd reach hungry children with food, medicine and other help, much faster. In other words, an airplane would save lives.

Our budgets were still very tight. Despite our new support from the United States, we were still barely making it from month to month. We spent the money as fast as it came in because so many children were suffering. It was a leap of faith to acquire an airplane, yet we believed that God would give us one to further His work—and He did.

We heard about a Piper Cherokee 6 that had been grounded in South West Africa (now Namibia), because the engine needed a complete overhaul. A friend, who was an aircraft technician, went to inspect the plane and reported that, other than a compression problem with the engine, it was in good shape. We made a ridiculously low offer of R25,000 (about $7,000 at that time).

It's been said that the two happiest days in a boat owner's life are:

1. The day he buys his boat, and
2. The day he sells it.

That's how the owners of this plane felt. It had become a big headache for them and they were happy to get rid of it at any price. We had a deal.

Our friend persuaded the authorities to allow him to fly the plane back to South Africa, even though they were reluctant because they thought the engine wasn't safe enough yet. Two hours into the flight, the engine began working perfectly. In Johannesburg, the craft underwent a thorough inspection, and there wasn't a thing wrong with it.

Another miracle!

We flew that plane more than 700 hours before we needed to overhaul the engine that had already been condemned. There is no limit to what God can or will do.

When I think back on those days, and how we used that little single-engine aircraft, I'm amazed at how God watched over us. That airplane was not fitted for instrument flight, and I was not instrument rated. That meant that when the weather was bad, we needed to fly at a very low level, just above the treetops, to see where we were going.

The countryside was full of armed rebels and they frequently took shots at us. It was so dangerous that the Red Cross aircraft that flew in and out of Beira on its relief missions had steel plates welded underneath the pilot seats to protect their pilots from rebel bullets. The rebels made no distinction between military aircraft and aircraft carrying relief supplies. They shot at everyone.

THROUGH ANN'S EYES

I was always nervous when we flew in that little plane. I remember one mission where we were gaining altitude, and I suddenly heard a loud noise in the back of the cabin.

Bang!

I screamed and ducked, sure that rebel gunfire had hit us. It turned out to be nothing quite so sinister. It was merely that the change in air pressure caused the top to pop off a large, plastic water bottle.

One reality of life in Mozambique was that no matter where we were, on the road or in the air, we were in danger of being shot.

We were constantly concerned about all those who had joined us in this work, knowing that they too faced danger every day. We had employed a family of four to run our orphanage and other work in Pambarra, where rebel attacks were common. It is one thing to put yourself or even your own family in danger, but it is something entirely different to know that you're responsible for placing another family in harm's way. Yet, even in this situation, it was a great comfort to know that God had brought all of us into Mozambique for a purpose, and that we were all where He wanted us to be.

Those early years in Mozambique were instrumental in helping us learn to trust God for our safety, and for the safety of those working with us. Our experiences there grew within us the ability to persevere even when all the odds were stacked against us. We learned that with God, all things are indeed possible to those who believe (Mark 9:23).

CHAPTER 12

DINING WITH PRESIDENTS

JOHANNESBURG, SOUTH AFRICA & WASHINGTON DC, UNITED STATES, 1986–1987

At first, our move to Johannesburg in 1986 was like starting over again. We bought land and needed to build offices and housing for our staff, many of whom now lived in little trailers. We brought in some of the prefabricated buildings we'd had on our property in Nelspruit, but we still had much work to do and it would be expensive.

I felt that God wanted us to move to Johannesburg because it was part of His plan for blessing and expanding our work. And that is exactly what happened. Donations flowed in from friends all over the world. For the first time, we felt that our tough "boot camp" days were over.

I suppose I should have known better than to think that we could become comfortable and complacent. After we had been in Johannesburg for a year, and things were looking good, someone asked me, "What are you going to do if your finances dry up?"

I could hardly believe it. What kind of question was that? Talk about a doubting Thomas! And yet, it made me realise that I had no idea what I'd do if the money stopped coming in. What would happen to all the hungry children who depended on us for their sustenance if our income was suddenly cut?

THROUGH ANN'S EYES

The move to Johannesburg was a challenge of obedience. Peter felt sure it was time for us to move from Nelspruit, in the beautiful peaceful countryside in the Lowveld, to the bustling city. This was a practical decision because access to services like additional telephone lines and availability of spare parts for maintaining our ever-growing fleet of vehicles made sense.

But it also meant leaving many of our closest friends who loved and supported us. These were some of the same friends who had seen our new life and calling unfold. I struggled with accepting the move for months. I had concerns about the city lifestyle, about finding new schools for our children and about the massive effort it would take to relocate our offices and team.

"I don't see how this can be God's will," I said to Peter. "God knows how much I love the Lowveld, and I've always said that I would never return to the big city."

Every move had been hard on me. We had moved from our beautiful farm to a small railway house. Then we'd moved to a property which included our offices in Nelspruit. I had received certain Scriptures that I took to be promises from God such as 2 Samuel 7:10—"they may dwell in a place of their own and move no more"—so I was sure that our days of moving had ended. God had other plans.

I finally accepted that our growth would be stifled if we remained where we were, so we needed to go.

Three months later we said goodbye to our beloved Nelspruit and headed for the big city. I cried many tears during those three months, but I was determined to obey.

Our precious team members were also being uprooted but agreed to come without complaint. Those people that God placed with us in the early days of our ministry were truly the salt of the earth. They went through so much with us. Their dedication and sacrifice helped lay the groundwork for an organisation that is today making a lasting, positive impact on millions of Africa's poorest children and their families.

THE PRESIDENT'S DINNER

Shortly after our move, a dear friend of ours, Tom Demery, invited us back to the United States for a second fundraising trip. He had arranged several dinners where we could present our work and, hopefully, line up the financial support we needed.

After one of these dinners, a man approached me and asked, "How would you like to have dinner with President Reagan?"

I waited for the punch line, but none came. He wasn't joking.

"What do you mean?"

"The President's Dinner is coming up soon, and I'd like you to come as my guests."

He explained that the Republican Party was about to host a dinner for 2,000 people in Washington D.C. on 29 April 1987; influential guests would accompany the President and Mrs.

Reagan, along with George and Barbara Bush and most of the members of the president's cabinet. Tickets were $1,500 apiece.

When I heard how much it cost, I'm sure my eyes bugged out. I wanted to be polite, but that was an awful lot of money for a dinner.

"We'd love to go to the dinner," I said. "But if it's all the same to you, we would rather have the money. Do you know how many children we can feed with $3,000?"

He shook his head. "I'm sorry, but I've already paid for the tickets."

There was no backing out. We would attend this black-tie event. We had no money for such an extravagance. Tom arranged for me to rent a tuxedo for the occasion, and his wife Carol provided a beautiful dress and costume jewelry for Ann. They even had us picked up in a stretch limousine.

That night when we strolled into the convention center on the red carpet, we felt like celebrities. The Lord has a great sense of humour. Anyone watching us as we strolled in like people of power and influence, movers and shakers in American politics, would never have guessed that we were two little missionaries from Africa who didn't even have two cents to rub together!

As we were escorted to our table, to my amazement, we kept getting closer and closer to the front.

It turned out that we were seated just three tables from the head table. I hadn't realised that the man who'd invited us to sit at his table had so much influence in Washington. We were so close that we could hear the President and Mrs.

Reagan speaking to one another. We recognised one guest as Piet Koornof, our South African Ambassador to the United States. He was two-thirds of the way to the back door. I'm sure he wondered how we rated such preferential treatment. When he heard we were from South Africa, he must have figured we were important people that he needed to know. Within 10 minutes, he was at our table chatting, and he then invited us to a "braaivleis" (barbecue) at his residence the following day. We politely turned him down, as we had already made plans to leave town by then.

A government official hosts each table at the President's Dinner. Alexander Haig was to be our host, but he became ill. So Maureen Reagan took his place.

I was so intimidated. What do you say to a president's daughter? I had no idea so, feeling completely out of place, I remained silent. I didn't even look at her. After a while, Maureen tapped me on the shoulder and said, "What do you do for a living?"

That was all it took to open the floodgates. Once I start talking about our work in Africa, I'm hard to stop. As I told her all about the heartbreaking situation in Mozambique, and what we were doing to save children's lives there, tears rolled down her cheeks.

"I love Mozambique," she said. "I've been there four or five times myself. What can I do to help you?"

"Oh, Lord, so this is why You wanted us to come to this fancy dinner? What a divine appointment!"

She reached into her purse, pulled out her business card,

and handed it to me. Until I looked at it, I hadn't realised that she was more than *just* the President's daughter, she was also vice-chairman of the Republican Party.

"Can you come to my office tomorrow?" she asked.

When I told her we were leaving town the following evening, she insisted that we come by first thing in the morning.

So that's what we did.

When I arrived, Ms. Reagan's secretary ushered us right into her spacious, beautifully furnished office. The intimidation I had felt the night before was gone. I could tell that Maureen was a genuine, caring woman who sincerely wanted to help the people of Mozambique.

Maureen got right to the point, "What can I do to help you?"

"It would be wonderful if you could help us raise some money for our work."

She nodded. "That's easy. What else can I do for you?"

I looked at Ann, and saw the sparkle in her eyes. I knew what it meant: *Don't hold back!*

"Well . . . " I took a deep breath. "I've been trying to talk to the State Department to see if we can get help from the United States government."

Her eyes narrowed. "You mean Chet hasn't been able to help you?"

"Chet? Who's Chet?"

"Dr. Chester Crocker," she said. "He's the Assistant Secretary of State in charge of African Affairs."

Ann already had a pen in hand, taking notes.

I smiled and admitted, "Maureen, I need you to understand

that I haven't even been able to get in the front door at the State Department, let alone talk to anyone in authority."

"You really have to talk to him." She picked up the phone and dialed. In moments, she was on his direct line. She recapped what I had told her about our work in Mozambique and asked Dr. Crocker if he had a few moments to talk to us.

"Yes, Chet," she said into the receiver, "I know you're busy. I understand. But you really have to meet these people." I could tell that he wasn't quite as enthusiastic as she was. "No, that won't work," she said. "They're leaving town later today. It won't take long."

He agreed to give us 10 minutes. We were whisked over to his office and, as it turned out, were there for over an hour.

Near the end of our time together, Dr. Crocker surprised us by saying, "I think you can help me."

"Us help you?" I asked. "How?"

He explained that a bill was pending before Congress that would help the frontline States affected by the sanctions placed on South Africa. Mozambique and Angola were excluded from this assistance because of their Marxist stand. The problem was that some right-wing Republicans had attached Mozambique's Food Aid to this bill. If this were passed, it would mean the loss of over $90 million in food aid.

"It would really help if you could testify before a Congressional Committee and another in the Senate, about what you are doing in Mozambique and the suffering you've seen there. Also, they need to know what would happen if this aid was withdrawn."

I readily agreed. "I'll be happy to do it."

So, that afternoon, this "little missionary from Africa" found himself testifying at two Congressional hearings. I told the U.S. legislators about the situation in Mozambique, and that it would lead to at least a million people starving to death if the food aid was taken away.

During the rest of our trip in the United States, we experienced one blessing after another and built several life-long friendships. One highlight for us was a fundraising dinner in Los Angeles, hosted by Maureen, where celebrities and movie stars contributed nearly $80,000 to help us feed the poor in Mozambique. Georgia Frontiere, owner of the National Football League's Los Angeles Rams, wrote a check for $16,000. The outpouring of support was incredible.

I remembered what God had told us, that He would use us as a conduit to channel help from people in America to suffering children in Africa. That's exactly what He was doing.

A CHANGE IN MOZAMBIQUE

Upon our return to South Africa, I sent a telex to Mozambique's Foreign Minister, telling him I had met with Dr. Chester Crocker in the United States. I provided no details, but said I'd like to meet with him to discuss the matter. Frankly, I hoped a little name-dropping might help us get the permission we needed to resume preaching in Mozambique. Perhaps Mozambique's rulers would sit up and take notice.

They did.

I received an immediate reply inviting me to come to

Maputo for a face-to-face meeting with the foreign minister. I was soon on my way.

When I walked into the Assistant Foreign Minister's office, he greeted me as if I were an old friend. He shook my hand warmly and said, "I really want to thank you for testifying before the American Congress." I hadn't yet told him about that, but I should have known that he would know. He continued, "What you did has helped us save the lives of many people. Thank you very much."

He asked me to sit down, and then he told me all about the policies of his government. Nobody in Mozambique had ever talked to me that way before. For the first time, I was being treated like somebody important.

As we sat talking, I noticed a dossier sitting on his desk with my name across the top. It was unnerving to see how thick the file was. Obviously, they'd been keeping close tabs on me from the first moment I set foot in their country. They probably knew everything about me, including what I'd told the members of the U.S. House and Senate.

My host explained, with a friendly smile on his face, that his government wanted to be on good terms with the United States, that their goal was to eradicate poverty and hunger in their country. He explained their economic policies and more, and the entire time I wondered why he was telling me all this.

Then it dawned on me. He thought I had pull with the American government. He wanted me to use my influence to improve Mozambique's standing with the Reagan administration. Of course, I didn't and I couldn't, but this was the opportunity I'd been looking for. I had to take it.

"Mr. Minister," I said, gaining his full attention. "I would love to speak on behalf of the Mozambican government, but there are a few things you need to understand."

"Yes?" He was all ears.

"First of all, Americans want to see a market economy. I can't really comment on that because I'm not an economist. But they also measure a country on whether there is freedom of religion, and you don't have that here."

His eyes narrowed. "What do you mean? We have those freedoms here."

"Then why can't I preach in Mozambique?"

"Preach?" He smiled. "You can preach here."

I shook my head. "No, I can't."

I reached into my briefcase and pulled out the letter I had received from the Minister of Justice, warning me not to even ask to hold another public outreach in Mozambique.

He glanced at the letter and sighed "I'll see what I can do."

Two weeks later, I received a telex from the Mozambican government giving us permission to hold three outreaches. What an amazing God we serve!

From that day forward, we were welcome in Mozambique. With newfound allies, our ministry had entered a new phase of rapid growth, and we were astounded by what happened.

Our next Mozambique outreach was in the city of Chimoio, in a public soccer stadium. More than 30,000 people came to the first night, which was a new attendance record for us. But by the end of our stay, the stadium was jammed full with

45,000 people or more every night. As always, God demonstrated the truth of His Word with thousands receiving Jesus and many dramatic healings.

Next, we returned to Beira, where we encountered an opening night crowd of more than 50,000. By the end of a week there, that number had grown to 70,000 or more. The people of Mozambique had an incredible hunger for God, and He was responding in dramatic fashion.

As a result of that one crusade, 82 new churches were established in the Beira area. It was an absolute joy to be a part of what God was doing, and this was only the beginning.

By God's grace, we developed a close relationship with the once-hostile government of Mozambique and felt strong affection for Joachim Chissano, who was then the Minister of Foreign Affairs. In October of 1986, Mozambique's President, Samora Moises Machel, died in a plane crash. Although saddened by Machel's death, we were delighted that our friend Mr. Chissano had been chosen as Mozambique's new president.

What a change from a few years prior! Back then, they had made it clear that we weren't welcome in Mozambique. Then I was warned that I would be arrested and thrown into jail if I attempted to preach the Gospel. Now, one of our *friends* was the Chief of State!

In fact, President Chissano officially opened our second outreach in Maputo. After addressing the crowd, he sat on our platform during the entire service. What a thrill it was to see the presidential motorcade making its way through the streets as he came to welcome us to the capital city. After the meeting, he joined our team in our catering trailer and spent time visiting with us.

Incidentally, in 1989, it was President Chissano who made the decision to abandon Marxism-Leninism and restore civil liberties in Mozambique.

How I wished that our troubles had disappeared and we would experience smooth sailing from that time forward, but that wasn't the case. Mozambique was still at war, and we were regularly surrounded by death and danger.

Nonetheless, we were so thankful. Working with a giant jigsaw puzzle, God had carefully positioned all the pieces to get us back into Mozambique. He always sees the big picture and works to bring it to pass.

In fact, for four years, I think we were the only Christian ministry allowed to hold public outreaches in that country. During that time, I preached the Word of God from the south to the north and in every city, exactly as God had promised.

CHAPTER 13

INTO THE FIRE

ANGOLA, SOUTH AFRICA, 1988–1992

From the moment Ann and I met James and Betty Robison in 1988, we realised that it was a significant, God-ordained moment—not only for us, but for the precious children of Africa.

James had heard that years ago we had helped an American pastor who had messed up, and that we had brought him to Africa to restore him and his family. That impressed James, and when he came to South Africa to speak at a conference, he searched us out saying, "I want to meet that man."

Right away, we found synergy in our hearts. I recognised at once that James Robison was a man who loved the downtrodden and the poor. He had a great heart of compassion.

On that trip, James advised us, "I want to start helping you immediately." And he did.

That was the beginning of a partnership that has lasted more than three decades and continues. It has enabled us to expand into the projects we have today. It also helped relieve our constant financial pressure and was the beginning of our understanding of what long-term strategic partnerships can achieve.

My friendship with James quickly grew into one of the most important relationships in my life. God gave me a brother and a buddy I could call on when I needed help, advice or just someone to talk to. I sensed that James would always be there for us. He told me often, "Peter, one day I will give you a million dollars a month for the children." I know that day is coming. Betty, James' wife, has also been a great friend and an encouragement to both of us.

With James' help we had one of our greatest breakthroughs we had ever had in our feeding projects. We established our own food factories where we now produce our own nutritious food much more effectively, milling the maize, processing soya beans and more, extruding and blending them together with vitamin and mineral additives into a highly nutritious porridge mix. As we converted to this feeding method, we found that our ability to feed hungry children multiplied exponentially. We would soon feed 65,000 children *every* school day.

These were the first steps of a new model for our nutritional feeding programs that have since spread throughout sub-Saharan Africa.

A VITAL LESSON LEARNED

With input from the Mozambique government, we came to realise that our feeding in the villages was keeping children from going to school. Nutrition without education does not change tomorrow. Effective education is not possible if someone is severely undernourished. It impairs one's ability to concentrate and learn.

Although most of the schools were held under a large, shady tree with a chalkboard propped up against the tree trunk, it was vital for the children to grow and learn. We moved our feeding to those outdoor schools and invited the parents and local community members to volunteer by collecting firewood and water to boil long enough to remove all impurities, then mixing with our pre-cooked powder. Their involvement was vital and continues to be so as they participate in bringing solutions to the hunger needs of their children.

THE WORST PLACE FOR A CHILD TO GROW UP

Things were running smoother, but as our work in Mozambique continued at full speed, we felt the need to expand into another one of Africa's most dangerous places: Angola.

Like Mozambique, Angola was a country in turmoil, with several armed groups fighting for control. South African troops had entered Angola in support of the National Union for the Total Independence of Angola (UNITA), and the two countries had been in a declared state of war for nearly 10 years.

A recent truce between South Africa and Angola gave us an opportunity to enter the country, but that didn't mean the fighting was over. The Soviet Union and Cuba, supporting a group called the Movement for the Popular Liberation of Angola, poured guns and weapons into the country. Meanwhile, the United States supported UNITA and another group called the National Front for the Liberation of Angola and UNITA. It was a confusing, dangerous situation, and the result was unbelievable misery for the massive needy population.

Before the fighting ended, more than 1.5 million people had been killed, and another 4 million lost their homes.

The situation in Angola was so bad that the United Nations said it was the worst place in the world for a child to grow up. I didn't see how any place could be worse than Mozambique, but I found that the people of Angola had experienced more tears, pain and sorrow.

I approached our friend, Joaquim Chissano, the President of Mozambique, and asked him to open the way for us to work in Angola. Mozambique and Angola were both previous Portuguese colonies and still had a good working relationship. He telexed the President of Angola, telling him of our work in Mozambique. Even though relationships between South Africa and Angola were still strained, we received an official invitation from the Angolan government to visit their country.

We did not know what to expect, nor did we anticipate all the challenges we would face in getting there. To prepare for our work there, we purchased a larger twin-engine aircraft. We needed this aircraft because Angola is a large country— nearly twice the size of Texas—and it is a lot further from South Africa than Mozambique. Furthermore, much of the land we would fly over was desert, so we needed a plane that could cover greater distances without needing to stop for fuel. It was also very dangerous to fly over Angola because both opposing sides had surface-to-air missiles and were prepared to use them. This became clear when they shot down the plane of the President of Botswana.

Before heading into Angola for the first time, we sent one

of our Portuguese-speaking staff members on ahead to the capital city of Luanda.

Even with our larger aircraft, we could not fly all the way from Johannesburg to Luanda in one hop. We had to make two stops, one in Windhoek, Namibia, then along the west coast because of the dangers of flying overland. We then needed to stop at Namib, a coastal town in southern Angola. We arranged with the government to have aviation fuel available, as our aircraft could not use jet fuel. When we arrived there, however, we discovered something we hadn't counted on: There was no fuel. Plenty of jet fuel was on hand, but nothing for a piston engine plane. Stranded in Namib, it looked as if we would never get out. We spent hours on the radio trying to figure out a way to get fuel from Luanda. Nothing seemed to work.

Finally, on the third day of our stay, we were surprised to see a large Antonov transport aircraft touch down on the Namib runway. That big plane taxied up, turned around and the back door opened. To our absolute joy, out stepped our staff member, a wide grin on her face. Inside that huge transport plane were three drums of Avgas, so we could refuel and fly on to Luanda.

Our trip hadn't started off on a good note, but all of that changed when we reached our destination. As we stepped off the plane in Luanda, we were shocked to see two Mercedes Benz limousines speeding across the tarmac in our direction. At first, we figured that some VIPs must be arriving. We were amazed to realise *we* were the VIPs!

President Chissano's telex had worked. Our visit to Angola

was considered "noteworthy" and we were treated well in every way. We were whisked away from the airport, skipping through the usual immigration lines, and taken to a hotel where the president's guests were accommodated. The media was in attendance wherever we went. What an incredible change from our early days in Mozambique, when we struggled to even have a meeting with the government!

In our first two days in Luanda, we met with many government ministers. High-ranking local officials awaited us everywhere we went. The media provided full coverage of our visit. It was obvious from the questions they asked that some people were suspicious of our motives. Only two months had passed since our two nations had signed a truce, and residual mistrust of South Africans still existed.

Fortunately, it turned out that the Angolan government displayed complete faith in us, and by the time we departed, we had signed a contract with them, giving us access to work wherever we desired. Within a few weeks of our arrival, we began feeding more than 20,000 children every day, and making plans for our first citywide outreach.

A BEWILDERED PEOPLE

It was in Angola, just like that life-changing day in Pambarra, that God again increased my understanding of the depths of His great compassion.

In parts of the world, Africa is perceived as a continent that always has its hand out, begging for help from others. But as I walked amongst the refugees that had been driven from their homes by the war, I saw a people who were bewildered, lost and hurting. Thousands of families lived in crowded, squalid refugee camps. They didn't have safe water, food, clothing or decent shelter. They had lost everything, including family members and others who they loved dearly. God showed me that this whole issue was about one thing: human beings who were oppressed and deserved a better life.

I believe that every child on this earth deserves a decent place to live and nutritious food to eat. It's not their fault that men are at war with each other, or that governments are inefficient or corrupt. We can't make decisions that hurt children just because their leaders carry out policies we don't like. We are called to minister God's love to everyone.

ONE VEHICLE IN GANDA

Once operating in Angola, we heard that many children were in a desperate plight in a place called Ganda.

We tried to fly our airplane loaded with food into Ganda but the only place to land an aircraft was a short, rutted dirt airstrip. Rain had turned it into a muddy swamp. On our way in, we hit stormy weather and turbulence tossed the aircraft here, there and everywhere. Finally, we turned around and returned to the city of Benguela. I couldn't give up, knowing that the situation in Ganda was so bad. I determined that nothing would stop us from reaching the starving children there.

Out of sheer desperation, we tried the impossible. We approached the Angolan Air Force to ask if there was any way we could charter a helicopter. We knew that the Air Force was unlikely to charter out their aircraft. Besides, the country was in the midst of a civil war and we were asking them to fly us into an area with intense fighting. To our surprise, the Air Force agreed and we loaded the chopper to capacity. Once we arrived in that desperate little town, we commandeered one of only two vehicles there and headed off to where we wanted to establish our feeding station.

We didn't make it far. Right in the middle of the town, the *only other vehicle* smashed right into us, totaling both vehicles. Thankfully, nobody was hurt.

Once again, our plans had hit a brick wall. That's when we discovered that there *was* one other motorized vehicle in Ganda . . . a tractor and trailer. The only problem was that the trailer was full of cow manure. I can't even describe the stench, but it didn't deter us. Starving children were waiting for our help. We climbed onto the trailer and tried not to breathe too deeply as we bounced along the terrible roads to the camp where the children were.

Upon arrival, we found that what we'd heard was true: the children were in a desperate condition, many starving to death. We fed them and left enough food to sustain them until we could return a few weeks later. Then, with the help of a little 50cc motorbike, we got our team back to the helicopter, one at a time.

Nothing is impossible with God! Something may be dangerous or difficult, but it is *never* impossible. If we had given up, turned around and gone home that day, many lives would have been lost. Without this nourishment, they would have been dead within days. But thank God, they survived!

WORK FOR FOOD

God loves the poor. I am so convinced of this. The places I have found the presence of Jesus to be the most tangible are places where most people wouldn't even want to go. We saw one great breakthrough after another in Angola. The European Union, through the Lutheran Federation, started supplying thousands of tons of food each year for distribution to be used for "work for food" projects. We re-opened a full agricultural irrigation system through this "work for food" support and re-established 16,000 people back to their farmlands where the vegetation soon looked like an oasis in the desert. In one year, we distributed over 8,000 tons of food and expanded our nutritional feeding.

My son, Isak, had a moving, personal experience of his own in Angola, with a baby named Matthew.

ISAK'S ACCOUNT

I walked into a malnutrition clinic we support in Benguela, Angola. "I hate these places," I thought to myself, as I entered the building. Is this what they mean when they talk about the smell of death? . . . not a vile smell, but rather the strange confluence of antiseptic, milk (from the therapeutic formula being used) and human body odor. Fearing to look down at the children lying on blankets on the floor, I prepared myself for the inevitable. The sight of children so malnourished that their little bodies are just skin and bone, feeding tubes inserted into their noses and a lifeless blankness in their eyes. This room was filled with lifeless and troubled souls.

I examined the children as their mothers watched my every move with great desperation. We exchanged no words, yet volumes of communication passed between these helpless mothers and myself. Then I saw him, Mateus Jamba (Matthew), a 2-year-old boy lying wrapped in a blanket . . . lifeless . . . dying. Matthew's face was so gaunt that his bones looked as though they could burst through his skin at any moment.

I asked his mother if I could open the blanket, and as I did, I wished I had not. The blanket revealed one of the worst sights I had yet witnessed in my life.

The smell of rotting flesh filled my nostrils, a sharp pungent smell. "My God, his skin is rotting off his body," I exclaimed. Large portions of his skin were literally falling off his body, his hands tied to stop him from scratching the skin off, revealing large open wounds. His ribs protruded to the point that they appeared as though they were above the skin. The nurses in the clinic tried to feed him small quantities of a therapeutic milk mix but to no avail. As they would inject it into the feeding tube, Matthew's painfully weak body would convulse, and he would vomit up the milk. I looked at one of the people with me and said, "There is no hope for him, he will die in the next few days."

We prayed for the young boy, and I recall thinking that only a miracle could save him. As we walked out of the clinic, I thought again how I hated these places.

Our trip ended, and as is necessary in our work, I put this

emotionally draining experience behind me and continued to do the best I could to meet the needs of those children who could be reached before getting into Matthew's condition. Then, a few weeks later, I received an email from our Angolan field base. The tone of the message was filled with a tangible excitement as it explained that Matthew had survived. He was not yet totally stable, but was doing much better. The next message told of how he had progressed from the therapeutic milk to a highly nutritious porridge provided to the clinic by *JAM*. This is always a great sign and normally means a child is now out of the critical stage.

When I returned to the same clinic, I was shocked to see who was waiting there to meet me . . . Matthew—not the Matthew I had seen dying just six months earlier, but rather a chubby, healthy young child. His mother had dressed him in his best clothes. I smiled at her and her face lit up. She said nothing, but her smile showed more gratitude than any words could express. I sat with Matthew on my lap, gave him candy and battled to contain my emotions as they showed me a picture of him as I had last seen him.

My mind wandered to those children who don't make it to the clinics, who we don't reach in time, who die as just another statistic. 'A child dies every eight seconds' is not just a statistic, but a human tragedy of epic proportions. What can we do to stop this, to bring about justice, a justice that sees no child die of starvation? We do what we are doing, we start with one Matthew at a time, gain back time, eight seconds at a time; we continue doing what we can do but on a much larger scale, until we reach our goal to feed millions of children every day.

It doesn't take much to provide a nutritious meal a day to a child like Matthew. Nothing elaborate, nothing complicated, simply a meal a day.

More donors are essential to our quest for justice for the Matthews of Africa—children who deserve a meal a day!

We need millions of partners around the world to step up and embrace the pain that poverty brings in order to make a difference and help these precious people.

WAR!

In 1992, Angola prepared for national elections, hopeful that peace would come at last. It was in this positive atmosphere that we held successful meetings in Benguela and Lobito, and then headed inland to Huamba. Crowds of 40,000 or more turned out every night, and God saved, healed and set many free.

During our time in Huamba, the first election results came out. The peace process unraveled. UNITA was said to have lost the election and the organisation's leader, Jonas Savimbi, was furious. "Fraud!" he proclaimed, and he ordered his followers to take up arms.

During the last couple of nights of our meetings, we saw tracer fire and heard heavy artillery. As I stood in front of huge crowds, preaching about the love of Christ, rockets lit up the evening sky all around the city. By closing night, the entire city seemed to be engulfed in the war.

The war had flared up so suddenly and with such savagery that it seemed we were stranded in Huambo. The airport was closed, now in the hands of the UNITA rebels.

We came up with a plan. We went to the airstrip the day before and told them we wanted to get something out of the aircraft. We made friends with the UNITA guards at the gate. The next day we returned and told them the same thing. This time we got into the aircraft, started the engines, took off and flew away, praying they wouldn't shoot us down. For the next two and half hours, we flew 100 feet above the ground to avoid missiles.

Tragically, more than 2,000 people who had accepted Jesus at our meetings were killed in the fighting before our teams could follow-up. As I grieved over their loss, I was comforted to realise that their salvation had come just in the nick of time.

FULFILLMENT

Though we made it out ourselves, our equipment did not. We left our gospel outreach rig in a churchyard for protection, but it was quickly destroyed. Soldiers took what they wanted and burned what remained. It was a huge loss, but it didn't take long before we were able to turn it for good. Truthfully, our equipment was inadequate for where we needed to go next. We used the opportunity to design and plan for a new rig, and God met our needs not through any one large donation but through multiple small donations from supporters all over the world. Within 12 months of our loss, we had a new rig, paid in full and ready to run. We used it for the first time in Mbuji Mayi, Zaire, now known as the Democratic Republic of Congo. On the first night, around 110,000 people turned out to hear the good news. On the final day, an unbelievable crowd of 280,000 attended.

As I gave the altar call on that last night, more than 111,000 people responded to surrender their lives to Jesus. I was overcome with emotion, not so much by the size of the crowd, but by the incredible fulfillment of the vision God had given me so many years before. I remembered back to that night on our tobacco farm in the Eastern Lowveld when God called me, only a few months after I had started serving Him, while I was still struggling with giving up cigarettes, when I was still copycatting other people's sermons. He promised me that I would see *tens and hundreds of thousands of people saved, even in one day.*

As I looked over the huge crowd, raising their hands to the sky, receiving new hope, I realised this was it.

This was that day.

The fulfillment of 'tens of hundreds of thousands of people saved, even in one day.'

Peter and his sister, Dawn, sitting side by side, always enjoying one another's company.

Peter and his father, mentor and best friend.

Ann's mother and father, Beryl and Jack Brown, in front of their beautiful family home with their five daughters and one son. Ann seated centre front.

Peter's eldest sons, Kevin (left) and Wade (right).

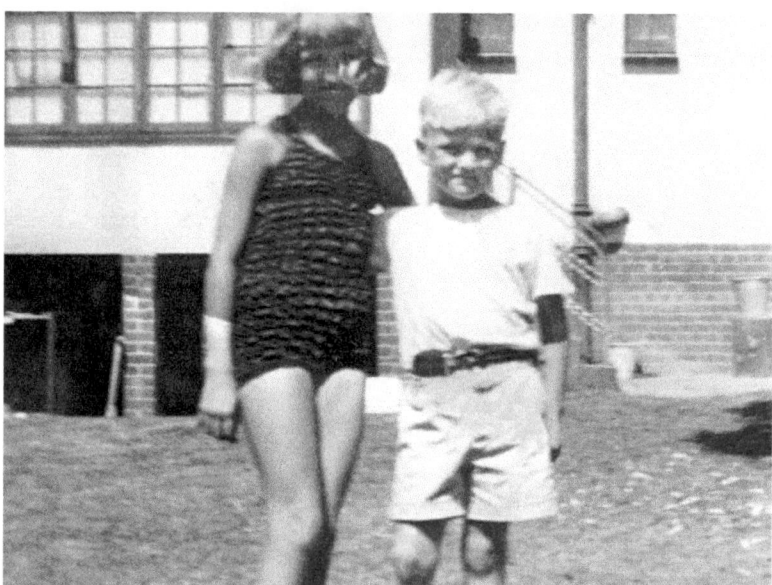

Peter with his sister, Dawn.

TUESDAY, FEBRUARY 11, 1958.

Established 1902
Registered at G.P.O. as a Newspaper.

Peter gets his scoop

When play stopped for drinks towards the end of the Springbok innings yesterday afternoon a young man with a camera, by name Peter Pretorius, suddenly dashed on to the field in the hope of getting a close-up picture. (Above) Peter gets his picture — of John Waite engaged in a chat. Having got his "picture of a lifetime" Little Peter, watched by Big Peter Heine, proceeds to leave the field (centre picture) even quicker than he had gone on. (Below): An incident in the play before Peter temporarily stole the limelight—Burke ducks in self-defence as McLean hooks Benaud to the boundary.

Thirteen-year-old Peter breaks the rules to get his photo!

Peter in front of his Formula 1 race car, before the race in Bulawayo, Zimbabwe.

Racing around the track at a speed of up to 168 mph. (Peter's car in front foreground).

May 1976, preparing breakfast on their honeymoon safari for his new bride.

Peter as 'wingman' to his son Wade, piloting an Impala jet fighter in the South African Air Force.

Peter's loving parents, Isak Jacobus Pretorius (above)
and Jeanette Catherine (S. Tee Geyser) (below).

Labourers working in the very labour-intense tobacco lands on Peter and Ann's "Pretoriuskop" farm.

In 1987, Peter and Ann leaving a meeting at the Government offices in Washington DC, USA.

An interesting news article about our work in Mozambique, printed in the South African Sunday Times national newspaper.

Jesus Alive Ministries' blue and white 5000-seater gospel tent.

Peter (pilot) and Ann (nervous passenger) alongside the 8-seater workhorse aircraft which made it possible to do the work in war-torn Mozambique.

Peter passionately preaching the gospel with power and anointing.

An enourmous crowd in the Democratic Republic of the Congo, eager to hear the Good News of the Gospel.

Hosted at the President's Dinner by Maureen Reagan, daughter
of President Ronald Reagan.

His heart breaking with compassion, Peter holds yet another fragile, malnourished baby. These experiences resulted in a growing determination to do more and more to prevent misery and death.

Peter and Ann (right) with James and Betty Robison (left). Many years, many experiences—many happy times shared with these faithful partners.

The fulfillment of bringing provision for those in need.
Peter and Ann (above); Peter and son, Isak (below).

Our beautiful six children in 1986. From left, front: Jackie, Tania, Grant, Isak.
Back: Ann, Peter, Kevin, Wade.

February 2015 Pretorius family at the celebration of Peter's 70th Birthday.
Top row in the tree: Tyler, Danielle, Kiera, Roxy, Terri, Jordan, Keenan, Peter
Bottom row: Tania, Jackie, Wendy, Grant, Terri, Isak, Peter, Ann, Wade, Nicci, Megan,
Belinda, Kevin.

PART III

NEVER ALONE

I thank my God upon every remembrance of you, always in every prayer of mine making request for you all with joy, for your fellowship in the gospel from the first day until now . . .

PHILIPPIANS 1:3−5

CHAPTER 14

"JESUS, I CAN'T DIE NOW!"

ANGOLA & RWANDA, SOUTH AFRICA, 1993–2014

I had just returned from a field trip in Angola and had enjoyed a wonderful evening with dear friends of ours, chatting about how well things were going in the organisation. Because of key partnerships, our work was growing, and it seemed we had turned the corner into yet another dimension.

Monthly support from James and Betty Robison's organisation, *Life Outreach International*, gave us a solid foundation and enabled us to expand, improve and even develop new projects. Talented and experienced people we had met in America now served on our Trustees Board and had become dear friends who had not only given generously themselves, but also helped us raise additional funds. Our institutional giving from the European Union increased, and we were excited about this new growth curve.

As we said goodbye, I suddenly felt a little strange, so I excused myself. When I walked into our bedroom, the most excruciating pain hit me in my chest. By the time Ann came in, I had collapsed onto the floor, writhing in pain. She hurriedly called our son, Isak. He helped me to the car, and they drove at high speed to the closest hospital. On the way, I remember panicking with the thought, "Jesus I can't die now! I'm not ready. There is still so much to do. What about my family and all the precious children depending on us?"

In the emergency room, I was immediately treated for a heart attack, then placed into the intensive care unit. I did not have a good night. The following day I was transferred by ambulance to another hospital for a catheterization. To everybody's amazement, the heart specialist could find no blockages or any cause for a heart attack. He thought it might have been a spasm in an artery, so he discharged me from the hospital. I didn't feel great, but I accepted his medical report.

Three days later, I flew our aircraft into Angola for a field trip as sole pilot with five passengers. While in Angola, the chest pains flared up again, so when I returned to Johannesburg, I returned to my doctor. He sent me for an abdominal scan; my gall bladder was full of stones. They removed my gall bladder, thinking this caused the pain. I felt better again, glad I could get back in the field.

But the chest pains continued. I chalked it up to recovering from gall bladder surgery and the intensity of my work schedule. I simply didn't have the commodity of time to recover, so I pushed on. I knew God was with me, but I did not realise just how much.

Several years later, we were on a trip to America and a friend encouraged us to go to a health clinic where they would sponsor a thorough medical exam, including a body scan. The health clinic immediately referred me to a heart specialist as the scan revealed a total blockage in one of my arteries. A catheterization confirmed that, in fact, one of my arteries had collapsed. Amazingly, my heart had somehow created its own bypass, using smaller veins in my heart to carry the necessary blood supply.

The fact that I had survived a heart attack and continued with a heavy schedule for months thereafter, was a miracle. It had left some damage as only 80% of my heart functioned normally. My heart specialist could not understand how the blockage was not diagnosed in South Africa. Cold chills hit me when I realised that I had piloted our aircraft, with passengers, in the midst of the heart attack—and that the chest pain had been my heart, desperately struggling to survive.

I learned again that I could trust God completely. Even when I don't know what's up, He does. This time I took the doctor's warning. I had seen over the past few years just what we could do with the help of the right partnerships—how we wouldn't have to struggle and how others could join in our vision, equally blessing them. That message had to get out to others so we could make an even greater impact. We were on the cusp of launching new programmes and partnership that would ensure that the changes we'd begun in Africa would continue far into the future, for generations to come. But some foundations still had to be laid.

"WE MUST DO WHATEVER WE CAN."

In April 1994, news of the genocide in Rwanda hit the media as Hutus slaughtered up to a million Tutsis in 90 days. Thousands of people fled across the border into the neighbouring area of Goma in the Congo.

I told Ann, "We must do whatever we can."

Laying foundations for situations like this required moving fast. Within days, Ann managed to secure funding from the European Union. They were delighted to hear that we were on the ground and available to assist the people immediately.

Our help began in the enormous Goma refugee camps, supplying and distributing food and clothing, with water provision, medical assistance and comfort. We found more than 100,000 "unaccompanied" children there. They didn't call them orphans in the beginning, but we knew that's what most of them were. A team of volunteers came from Norway to partner with us, extending our outreach. They worked tirelessly day and night, helping with whatever needs arose.

We were among the first to enter Rwanda directly after the genocide. We were able to get into the Gitarama province, then travelled up to Rwanda's capital, Kigali, which was—to our horror—a ghost town. There we found dead bodies floating in the lakes, laying alongside the roads and heaped in buildings. Large trucks loaded and transported the bodies away. Hundreds of children were displaced, separated from their families in the flurry for survival from their attackers. They were desperate and confused.

We found a man by the name of Fred Nkunda, who was taking care of hundreds of these children, but with little or no resources.

With a broken heart, I called James Robison and described the immense and desperate need that had arisen. I asked for whatever help his organisation could offer. Knowing that his viewers would respond, James agreed to not only help, but to fly over so he could witness first-hand the plight of the people.

When he arrived and I introduced him to Fred, James didn't hesitate. He echoed the words that were still on my heart. "We must do whatever we can. We can do this together." At once, all of us, including James' film crew, emptied our pockets. After more work, James returned home to raise additional funding to provide food and shelter for those precious children.

We secured temporary shelter in a Catholic compound and, over the next two years, we built a beautiful orphanage to house and care for more than 700 orphaned children. We provided work opportunities and skills development as teams hand-manufactured bricks from local clay alongside the nearby river. Thirty-seven widowed "mothers" took care of the everyday needs of the children, while other staff maintained the property, prepared meals and assisted in daily recreational activities.

On one of our visits to the orphanage, Ann and I interviewed several of the children, encouraging them to tell us their story. It was heart-wrenching to hear of the atrocities they had experienced as most of them witnessed their parents being hacked to death with machetes. Many of them banded together and hid in the forests, digging up roots that they ate raw, not chancing being seen with a fire.

When asked how they survived, they proudly exclaimed in their local Kinyarwandan language, "Because we can run very fast!"

Tears ran down Ann's face, and those brave little souls looked at her, curious at her sadness. When she asked how they felt about it now, they gestured and said, "That was then."

We were astounded how those children, and hundreds of others who found themselves in the same plight, could put such terrible experiences behind them. We concluded that one of the most important ingredients for their survival was an atmosphere of love. Through gently reaching out to them with the message of the Gospel, most of them accepted Jesus and found new hope.

Over the next decade, we fostered more than 12,000 children into Rwandan homes through this orphanage named the "Fred Nkunda Life Center," named in honour of the man we originally met who had selflessly taken care of so many of those displaced children. Once all the orphans were educated and relocated into Rwandan society, the centre transitioned into a skills development project, providing much-needed training for young men and women. This is its continued mission today.

HELPING AFRICA HELP ITSELF

When I look back at all the Lord has done through this ministry, I am humbled and awed, amazed and honored. Who would have thought that a South African adrenaline junkie who had known both wealth and poverty, who had made countless youthful mistakes, who had made his living in tobacco, would have been chosen by God to reach out to Africa. Yet, here I am. Forty years later, and I've seen God work miracles in ways far beyond my wildest imagination.

I've had the privilege of preaching the Word to millions and seeing tens of thousands accept Christ in a day. I've seen the Scripture come alive as the blind receive new eyes, the lame stretch out their legs and dance, the hungry fill their bellies and the hurting receive healing.

Much of what I saw happened in large meetings, but within the last decade, the Lord put it on my heart to go outside of the cities and into the rural villages. We researched and found that 57% of Africans live in rural villages over 20 kilometres away from a city. In those places, the Gospel is absent. Many of those people have heard of the Bible and Christianity, but they've never had the Gospel preached to them. This has become our new mission field.

When we go into a village, not only does the whole village come to our meetings, but also those from surrounding villages. Time and again, the number of people who give their lives to Jesus is greater than the population of the village we go to!

In fact, I became so impressed with the result of going to the rural communities that we started training ministers who had been a part of our outreach preparation teams, to reach out and evangelise to the villages themselves. And have they loved it! Rather than depending on me, each trained minister partners with an assistant to take the Gospel to the people of their country, rural district-by-district. The results have been miraculous and exponential, with those who hear the Gospel, continuing to share the good news themselves.

We even started holding outreaches in the rainy season,

which challenged our teams to use their faith for clear skies during each meeting. I'm proud to report that they have done extremely well as God has responded to their faith! Every day, our teams in the Congo, Tanzania and Kenya are not only helping people make decisions for Jesus, but they are training up new ministers and evangelists to replicate the process, therefore multiplying our efforts. It is more than we could have imagined, but God certainly imagined it. He directed it, and He blessed it. As of 2018, we've had 2.7 million registered decisions for Jesus in the villages . . . and the number continues to grow!

NUTRITIONAL FEEDING

Our nutritional feeding program may have started with feeding 20,000 children per day in Mozambique, but now 35 years later, we feed more than *1.2 million children every day* in four countries. I never get tired of hearing that—*1.2 million children fed every day*. Ann and I recently calculated that since that first outreach in Pambarra, Mozambique, our nutritional feeding program has served over 1.2 *billion* meals.

What began with nutritional feeding transitioned into "school feeding." Children were in the habit of coming to us for food, but we wanted to give them more than a meal. We wanted to give them a future, so we tied our nutritional feeding to primary schools. Now, children come to receive nourishment *and* an education.

In Mozambique, as of 2013, more than 300,000 children receive a "Red Bowl" in our school feeding model. Even better, the food used is home grown. It is produced in and around the school.

What began in Mozambique, we continued into Angola. In 1991, those operations began with relief feeding in the province of Benguela but we quickly transitioned them into school feeding, a model that continues to this day. As of 2013, we feed more than 220,000 primary school children every day in the provinces of Benguela and Kwanza-Sul.

In 2002, we expanded our nutritional feeding into South Sudan, then still part of the country of Sudan. Once again, civil war had caused massive displacement of Sudan's citizens. Our partners helped us provide food for those in need of relief feeding. In time, we duplicated our school feeding program. As of 2011, 500,000 children receive nourishment every day.

Then in 2004, the Lord directed us to bring a duplication of our efforts back home to South Africa. Poor neighbourhoods in our own country suffer from poverty and hunger, too. The result is hungry children who are at risk for earning poor scores at school and turning to the streets to provide what they are unable to find elsewhere. So when the South African government took over primary school feeding, we began to provide meals to preschool children.

With the help of our partners, we went into informal settlements in poor communities with rudimentary childcare facilities and transformed them into bright, lively schools where children receive nutritional feeding and quality educations with trained teachers. These schools once were little more than corrugated iron tin shacks that were extremely cold during the winter. They leaked during the rainy season and became ovens during the summer. Parents in those areas often had no other option—but today, more than 62,000 preschool students receive meals and education at schools in Gauteng, Eastern and Western Cape, KZN and Limpopo.

Only God knows what the future holds. We never could have imagined that God would have used the 10 days I was stranded in Pambarra to light a fire in us to feed more than a million children every day . . . and yet, that is exactly what the Lord has done.

WATER AND SANITATION

When we travelled to rural areas, I noticed that the women spent much of their day collecting water. They carried jugs, cans, buckets and anything else they could find to collect water from sources that were little more than mud holes. The water was full of bacteria and parasites and a whole host of contaminates that led to deadly diseases like cholera and typhoid.

For people living in first world countries, clean water is common, but, in fact, the World Health Organization estimates that every year 1.75 million children around the world die from water-borne diseases. Ninety percent of those deaths are children under five years of age. A good portion of those deaths occur in rural Africa where access to clean, safe water is rare.

When I heard those statistics and saw first-hand the deaths and sickness associated with contaminated drinking water, and when I witnessed the women collecting water, I knew our ministry had to be part of the solution. In 2001, we purchased drilling rigs and started drilling for clean water. By 2013, we had drilled 2,500 wells of clean water in South Africa, South Sudan, Angola, Mozambique, Ethiopia and Zimbabwe. Each well serves 1,000 people and can make a lasting impact on the community. It can mean the difference between life and death.

We approach all of our programmes mindful of tomorrow. We might start in answer to an immediate, dire need, but we strive to reach beyond the present and affect the future. Our water and sanitation efforts are no different. We train the community in sanitation procedures and proper water usage so that every well can last longer and serve that community to the fullest extent.

AGRICULTURAL DEVELOPMENT

One of our highest priorities for "Helping Africa Help Itself" is agricultural development. We tailor our agricultural projects to the area they serve. In partnership with *Life Outreach International*, in Mozambique we have established a large demonstration farm that helps community farmers see the potential in the land and trains them in farming techniques. South Africa has 600 active projects that teach famers the skills they need as well as provides them with tools, seeds and fertiliser so they can be successful. Twenty-one projects exist in South Sudan where we have partnered with the World Food Programme to establish community gardens, nurseries and livestock projects.

Often the food grown through these projects is used in the nutritional feeding's porridge. That means that food raised in

Africa is being used to feed Africans. Just imagine what it will mean to the African people when they have the means and knowhow to feed themselves. No longer will the world perceive Africa as always having its hand out. Instead, it will be in the position of caring for itself. That will be a fulfillment of our vision of "Helping Africa Help Itself."

TWO MINISTRIES, LIKE VISIONS

In 2004, we separated our gospel and our humanitarian work. *Jesus Alive Ministries* focuses on preaching the gospel message and our humanitarian work operates under *JAM (Joint Aid Management, International)*, demonstrating the Good News message of love and compassion.

We have transformed from being one organisation, driven by a pioneering spirit, into two organisations. We have a well-trained, global staff of around 500 people, operating in various countries, with good operational systems to take us into the future.

In *Jesus Alive Ministries*, with the help of translators from all over sub-Saharan Africa, we spent 12 years developing a strong follow-up teaching project that includes 50 hours of discipleship teaching, translated into 64 different languages. Through our outreaches, we have seen more than 12 million people respond to receive Jesus.

At the time of writing this book, *JAM* is helping Africa help itself by:

- Feeding more than 1.2 million hungry children through the educational school-feeding platforms.

- Assisting to improve education in schools.
- Drilling over 200 water wells each year.
- Helping families affected by HIV/AIDS through established projects and wonderful partnerships.
- Working to establish community-based agricultural projects and farmer training as well as vegetable gardens in schools and rural communities.
- Developing sustainable projects with opportunities in agriculture, food preparation, food factory operations, logistics, driving, mechanics, project assessments, monitoring and evaluation.

We continue to expand into other countries as we help the poor in Malawi, Democratic Republic of Congo and South Sudan. We also assist with relief supplies and projects in Zimbabwe and Ethiopia. With a signed contract with the Government of Sierra Leone, we are embarking on new ventures in yet another nation as we continue "Helping Africa Help Itself."

THROUGH ANN'S EYES

Despite the success the Lord has brought us, the enemy hasn't let up.

For instance, in March 2014, while Peter and I were attending a Global Conference in Panama, my phone rang at 6 a.m. Our daughter, Jackie, who lives on our mission base, was in a panic, "Mom, please tell me what to do. There are men with guns here. I left to collect the girls from school, but as I approached the gate, a man with an assault rifle aimed it at me. At high speed, I reversed the car all the way up the driveway until I could turn into Dad's office entrance. The door is locked, and I'm hiding in Dad's carport. Please tell me what to do!"

I tried to calm her as I forced myself through the heavy cloud of jet-lagged sleep. "Stay where you are, my precious. Try to keep calm."

My mind buzzed as I tried to think how the professionals on 911 handled emergencies like this. I made one or two phone calls then called her back. She still cowered behind her car in the carport, fortunately out of harm's way.

What had transpired was a military-style, well-orchestrated attack with three separate groups of armed men—each group dispatched to a different office block. Those in our main block smashed through the wooden security-enforced doors in our reception area and went directly to the office of Angie, our Financial Director, where she and Barry, our VP of Water Services were meeting. One man hit Barry on the head with the butt of his gun, knocking him unconscious. The other man demanded money. Angie offered him R1000.00 in cash, which he threw back at her. "We want U.S. dollars!"

The second group were in our *JAM* South Africa offices holding our team there at gunpoint, demanding cellphones, iPads and watches, while their accomplices dragged the secretary upstairs to where the safe was. Fortunately, the safe was empty, as they had banked earlier that morning.

The third group were stationed at our entrance gate, holding at gunpoint all those who arrived.

It was the surprise arrival of Jackie, wanting to exit at the gate that caused them to run. The men in Angie's office had the gate in their line of sight and called on their radio, "Red alert! Red alert! The silver car is free! Get out of here!" All three groups converged at the entrance and hit the road at top speed.

Although several of our staff tracked them on their missing iPads and phones, the police were unable to close in or apprehend them.

Many of our team were unnerved by this experience, but we are all grateful that nobody was killed. Barry recovered well from his hit on the head, and no substantial amount of cash was on hand. We were fortunately able to reinforce and upgrade our security systems through generous contributions of several donors. But we're reminded that every day threats remain.

"BECAUSE YOU WILL GO."

Dietrich Bonhoeffer said that one of the marks of a disciple of Christ is that he doesn't know for sure where he's going. All he knows is that he is following Christ.

That was exactly how it was for us. Many times, I wished God would let us know what the future held. But perhaps it's best that we didn't know, because we probably would have spent far too much time fretting.

What would we have done, during those early days in our tobacco church, if we had known that God planned to lead us into the middle of a war zone in Mozambique? Would we have turned and run the other way? Perhaps.

Then even after we were in the thick of our ministry in Mozambique, we had no way of knowing that one day we would be led into other regions ravaged by war, violence, hunger, sickness and intense suffering—like Angola and then the 1994 genocide in Rwanda. Yet God always knew when we were ready for the next step.

Along the way, there were certainly times when I longed for an easier, stress-free life. On one of those occasions I asked God why He sent us into such tough, war-torn and dangerous places.

His response was not what I wanted to hear. He simply said, "Because you will go."

YOU ARE OUR PARTNER

As we wrote this book, we relived the history of God's fingerprints on every moment of our lives, even long before we knew Him. In my younger years, I raced cars, flew planes and loved the rush of defying death. That ability to stare death down has served me well in this calling. Even owning a tobacco farm taught me valuable farming lessons that have helped our ministry help the people of Africa.

Looking back, it's so clear to me now how God has used my experience and my drive to create everything He's placed into this ministry today. Perhaps this will inspire you to look back at your own life and experiences, even the negative ones, and see God's hand turning around your mistakes for His good.

That's the way God works. He doesn't dismiss us because of our imperfections. He molds us—failings and all—into the world-changer He's called each of us to be. As you've seen, it can take time. I was saved for five months when God told me I would preach to hundreds of thousands of people, and even see a hundred thousand get saved in one day. It took 18 years for that to happen, but God knew it was coming. He put that vision in my heart even when I hadn't yet preached to 500 people!

If you are tempted to think that I am in some way "special," let me assure you that I am no different from you. I am very real and very human. I have had my challenges, some of them frightening and seemingly impossible to overcome. Over the years I have done many things in fear and trembling, but I have also learned that with God nothing is impossible. In Him, we really are more than conquerors. If you persevere, God will take you through.

The truth is that all of us can be used as God's instrument of love. We are His hands as we respond to His heart. Not all are called to go to the heart of darkness in Africa, but we are all called to make a difference for others in this world.

Perhaps as you've been reading you wonder what God's calling for your life is. Maybe you wonder how you, too, can change hundreds of thousands of lives every day.

As the Body of Christ, we are called to work together, each of us contributing a valuable part of what Christ is doing through us as a whole. I firmly believe that this ministry has grown and changed so many lives, not because of what I've done, or because of what Ann has done, but because of the valuable partnerships God has brought into our lives—and that includes people like *you.*

People just like you catch this vision each and every day. It's a vision for the whole Body of Christ, and partnerships like yours are the heart and soul of this ministry. He may be calling you to work with us on site, to bring your creativity to our outreaches or to carry on the valuable ministry of helping fund this expensive work. However He's calling you, I believe He has a place for us together. This has never been something we could do alone. We need people like you, *especially* people like you, who have read our story and completely comprehend this burden the Lord has put on our hearts for the people of Africa . . . to feed them, to educate them, to clothe them, to equip them and to save them.

THROUGH ANN'S EYES

The involvement of our children in our mission has resulted in a great impact on their hearts and their personal values. As a mom, I am so happy to see how they love one another and how God has made us a close and caring family. I am proud to see how deeply they care for others and how this is passing on to their beautiful children, who love our work and spread the word—and even provide an opportunity for their friends to also join in the fight against poverty and lack.

Although Wade enjoyed the exhilaration of flying jet fighter planes and military helicopters, then later large passenger airliners, he assisted us when he could by flying our little six-seater airplane. Kevin was involved for several years in helping our team set up our various food factories and their production lines. Tania has found ways in her busy schedule to raise awareness and funds through her social and church circles, as well as through her children's schools. Grant, as he was studying his accountancy degree, with his brilliant mind for numbers, assisted our Finance Department during his holidays.

For sixteen years, Isak served faithfully in every department of our ministry, learning all aspects of the organisation, and worked his way up to a leading role. He is convinced that, alongside humanitarian assistance, the long-term solution for the alleviation of poverty is to provide skills development through commercial investors participating in business opportunities on the continent of Africa. This is what he is currently pursuing.

Jackie, with an accountancy degree and equal gifting in creative design, has fully participated in our mission, and now serves alongside us in a leadership role.

ARE YOU READY?

Are you interested in changing this world? Then there's a place for you with us. As you've seen in these pages, God uses ordinary people like you and me to do extraordinary things. It's our giftings working together, complementing one another for one common purpose, that makes a difference. By utilizing and extracting strength from each other, we become a formidable force . . . together with God!

Please go to JAMInt.com and JesusAliveGO.org now and join our mailing lists so you will receive regular updates about exactly what you can pray for—because your prayers are invaluable to us.

Then, as the Lord leads you, please set up a recurring

contribution to join our efforts. Funding is the life-blood that keeps our work going and enables people from all over the world to take hands and join hearts with us in this amazing partnership that brings a brighter future for precious souls in need.

I know that if we're going to really help the poor, we will have to partner with people—friends all over the world like you—who understand what we're trying to do and have a heart for the poor themselves. That's how this ministry started. That has always been the strength of *JAM*.

We're looking forward to the next generation taking up this cause, not letting what God has done through us die, but rather *grow* and reach more people than we've even seen in our lifetime.

Passing this vision on to you is our legacy.

IT'S NOT OVER UNTIL IT'S OVER

JOHNANNESBURG, SOUTH AFRICA, 2015

In September of 2015, at a routine check-up with my cardiologist, he felt it wise to do additional tests. Unfortunately, these revealed the need for triple bypass heart surgery, which would take place a few days later. As I was wheeled into the operating room, I prayed, "Jesus, I am in your hands, and I know that You are more than able to take care of me."

THROUGH ANN'S EYES

After seven hours of surgery, with my family sitting alongside me in the hospital waiting room, we were relieved to hear that all had gone well and once the specialist surgeon had settled Peter in the intensive care unit, we could enjoy a short visit. The hospital staff had briefed us as to what to expect after heart surgery, but nothing could have prepared us for what we were about to experience.

Suddenly, we could sense panic as staff ran back and forth between the ICU and the operating rooms. Time was of the essence. It was more than seven hours later before the surgeon was able to sit with us and explain what had happened. Within ten minutes of being wheeled into the ICU, Peter's blood pressure dropped dramatically, and his heart stopped.

The surgeon could not take any time to get him back into the operating room and, as he put it, "I ripped his chest open again, smashing his ribs to get to his heart as quickly as possible."

He discovered that blood had coagulated all around Peter's heart. It was too thick to pump so it had seized up. Taking his heart into his hand, the surgeon gently pumped his heart as he carefully syringed the thickened blood out with a sterile saline solution. This took at least 45 minutes, during which time Peter was clinically dead and his extremities and all his organs and brain were without blood flow and oxygen. They later placed him on a heart-lung machine that kept him alive for the next five days.

Unfortunately, his kidneys came under enormous strain and also failed. He was in "multi-organ failure" and was kept immobilised and unconscious for 12 days.

Our children were amazing. Each of them in their own unique way encouraged one another. I marveled at the goodness of God who has made our disjointed family one very special unit who love and care for each other. I recalled the years and countless times we reminded one another that if we referred to each other with the prefix "step," we would surely trip on it. For me to receive their great tireless support and understanding overwhelmed me. It was very hard for us to see our giant of a man immobilised and lying unconscious day after day. The only change we saw was the growing stubble on his unshaven face. His body was so badly swollen that they needed to tape his unblinking eyes closed.

One of our most anxious moments was on day five when the surgeon needed to remove the heart lung machine which would require Peter's heart to operate on its own. The children and I held hands in a circle, asking God to be in charge and bring him through. Thank God, He did.

It was two weeks before his weakened body responded as he came out of the coma, having fought off infection after infection. We were delighted when we saw the first smile as he responded to Wade's voice.

The hospital staff were wonderful, and even permitted our grandchildren to visit. They noticed Peter's improvement when he heard and recognised their voices. The children always loved observing Peter's dancing eyebrows as he concentrated when they spoke to him, so when Casey-Lee, one of our granddaughters was visiting and asked 'Oupa' if he could still do the 'eyebrow dance', there were screeches of delight as his eyebrows gyrated up and down. What a relief to see him respond!

It was a long and difficult 32 days that Peter lay in the ICU, fighting for his life as infection tried to take over, but slowly his lungs then kidneys began to function unassisted again.

There were many moments when I wondered if there was damage to his brain from the prolonged lack of blood flow and oxygen. He had no concept of time, was often very confused, experienced double vision and did some strange things.

Then suddenly, on 6 October 2015, he went into cardiac arrest. Electric shocks with paddles administered by an ICU specialist, who was close by at the time, resuscitated him.

THE VISION IS STILL ALIVE

As I regained consciousness over several days, I realised I was in a massive spiritual battle to keep going. I think it was harder on my family than it was on me. They knew that there could be severe brain damage and other serious results from the multi-organ failure that my body experienced. Yet they continued to believe that Jesus would bring me through. They were there for me, and one another, in a way that only a close-knit family can be, sharing long hours of vigil at my bedside.

I lay in my hospital bed, thankful for the ability to think. I could have so easily been brain-dead. Yet as time dragged on, all I thought about was getting out of the intensive care unit that held me captive. Day and night were the same. The lights stayed on and the peep, peep, peep of the machines never ended. Sleep eluded me.

I praised God that at least I had familiar voices at my side helping me make it through. I cherished the moments my precious grandchildren massaged my hands or played with my hair. It brought me new hope and determination.

Yet my thoughts were not just about survival and my family. They were also about getting back to the work God had called me to do. Images of the children we served flashed into my mind. The millions of dependents waiting on the other side of my healing drew me to get stronger day by day.

I prayed, "Jesus, I don't only want to survive, I want to see growth. I am not done yet; I want to be a part of developing this organisation further, preparing it for the future and handing it over to the next generation."

My cardiologist entered the room and stood at my bedside. He didn't mince words. "With all your body experienced, you shouldn't be alive." My grandchildren should have been prepared to say good-bye to their Oupa.

"I've decided to rename you 'MM,'" the doctor stated with a smile. "That stands for 'Miracle Man.' You have restored my faith to know that God still performs miracles."

His words brought me back to that moment in 1979 when I received an unexpected phone call about my own father in the hospital, suffering from a heart attack. I remembered how we wanted more time with him, more time for his grandchildren to call him Oupa, and how—by nothing short of a miracle—we received it. Back then, my father was the Miracle Man whose restoration brought about a change in me and led to four decades of death-defying faith.

Today, I stand before my own children and grandchildren, completely restored, and hope that the miracle God has created in me resonates in their lives . . . and in yours . . . to approach God with a simple faith to just believe that He will do all He says He will do. I hope you see that He's in the business of using ordinary people to do extraordinary things.

And I'm not done yet. My heart beats with a powerful drive to finish my race yet still. My life was not taken, and the vision, dream and calling are still alive, stronger than ever. Together, for the remainder of my days, and far beyond, with your partnership, we are helping our beloved Africa help itself. ❖

FINISHING THE RACE

But none of these things move me; nor do I count my life dear to myself, so that I may finish my race with joy, and the ministry which I received from the Lord Jesus, to testify to the gospel of the grace of God.

ACTS 20:24

ACKNOWLEDGEMENTS

Partners and friends have been vital to us and have had a marked effect on our journey. Ann and I have never chased after money. Sure, we have asked people to help us, but what has been most important to us is to build relationships with partners who would walk the journey with us.

We will always honour our dear friends **Rodney and Nita Lloyd** who opened the way for us to visit the United States, resulting in many, many doors of opportunity. Also **Tom and Carol Demery,** who we met on our first trip to America and who have remained faithful friends, giving input and praying diligently for us over three decades; as have many churches, pastors and leaders from around the world, who have faithfully invested into our mission each month.

James and Betty Robison have walked together with us as development partners in Africa since 1988. This is one of the main reasons we have been able to get as far as we have. We have become good friends, having shared much of the dirt and grime, alongside one another, sleeping in a grass and reed hut in Mozambique or in converted shipping containers in Angola. Always together, with the same compassion beating in our hearts, while their *Life Outreach International* film crew have been actively capturing the story of all that we passionately share together.

Al Simon, whom we also met in the 1980s, was one of my

closest friends for many years. There was nothing that I could not ask him. He initially came from America to assist us in Africa for a number of months, and enjoyed learning the various aspects of our work while doing whatever we could give him to do. I have so many fond memories of tough situations and projects that Al assisted us with. One of these was when a group of our team, including a US citizen, were arrested in Kenya. Al immediately contacted a friend and Congressman who was able to assist in having them released. On another occasion, when several of our team were stranded during the war in Brazzaville Congo, the French Foreign Legion rescued them. Once again it was Al Simon who came to the rescue. I could call Al in the middle of the night. "Just give me a few minutes," he would say, and he immediately sprang into action. With the pressures of working in many troublesome areas, I needed a friend like him. Unfortunately, just before the Christmas of 2007, Al suddenly passed away from heart failure. To this day, I miss him greatly and am blessed to enjoy his wife **Susie's** involvement with us along with their wonderful children, **Suzannah and Christopher**.

Tom and Laurie Cunnington have been amazing friends who have also "walked the road" with us for over 30 years. This couple has helped us to raise substantial funds for the children of Africa; but, there has always been much more than that in our relationship. We enjoyed many fun times together on their trips to Africa and our trips to America, and they have always cared for us personally. We have prayed each other through health and other challenges, always emerging on the other side with the help of God. Friends like these really do share your family and your world together, even though thousands of miles separate you. We appreciate them.

Pastor Ray McCauley has been our pastor since 1987, and always a great encouragement to us. He has always acknowledged our calling and mission, guiding us in God's wisdom while faithfully supporting us and spurring us on. Our friendship has continued to deepen over these many years and especially in the last few years as he and I both faced challenges with our health. We have stood together, serving the Lord with gladness.

Dr. Pat Robertson is another faithful friend who, over the years, has always been delighted to meet with us and willingly support our gospel outreaches. Ann and I have enjoyed many stimulating and interesting discussions with him and his dear wife, **Dede**.

And, of course, this section wouldn't be complete without mentioning **Reinhard and Anni Bonnke** who have been mentors, encouragers and friends throughout our journey.

Over the many years on our mission, there are those who can "see the vision" with you and walk closely beside you. And there are many who give a lifetime of faithful service with you. We have several team members and their families who have worked shoulder-to-shoulder alongside us for several decades. They are true heroes and wonderfully valuable to our mission, as they implement and fulfill what God has given us to do. We honour and greatly appreciate them.

We have enjoyed building close friendships and relationships with amazing individuals from different walks of life, on different continents of the world. Each of these have enriched our lives in many different aspects, while spurring us on in all that we do, now as a global organisation.

—Peter & Ann

THROUGH ANN'S EYES

Shortly after this book went to print, my dear husband, Peter, passed away. In the midst of immense grief over such a tremendous loss, I celebrate the life of my husband and the race he so faithfully ran. Peter's message of faith was simple: God uses ordinary people to accomplish extraordinary things. As you've read, his life was truly a testament to this. I pray this book touches everyone who reads it to live with the same faith that Peter did, believing that God would do all He says He will do.

Peter has touched the lives of so many, and I know his legacy will continue doing so for years and years to come. Peter loved adventure, and I believe he has just embarked on his greatest adventure yet. Psalm 16:11 says, "You will show me the path of life; in Your presence is fullness of joy; in Your right hand there are pleasures forevermore" (AMP).

God showed Peter and me the path of life and took us to places we never imagined. We shared so many joys on this earth together, and now, Peter has finished his race and is in the presence of the Jesus he loves, where there are pleasures and rest forevermore. What a joyful day in heaven it will be when we are reunited, but until then, we will continue running the race that Peter started.

There are still so many in need, and though Peter is gone, his love for the continent of Africa remains in me, our family, our staff and all the lives that he touched. **The vision is still alive.**

Thank you, Peter, for the decades of love, adventure and faith. We miss you so greatly.

—Love always, Ann

JOIN THE VISION AND MAKE A DIFFERENCE—TODAY.

HELPING AFRICA HELP ITSELF

JAMInt.com

....

Gospel Outreach

with Peter Pretorius

Jesus Gospel Outreach
Taking the gospel to the poor.
JesusAliveGo.org